THE MOVING TREES

Diary of a Khe Sanh Marine

By JAMES C. OYSTER

© 2011 James Oyster
All Rights Reserved.

No part of this publication may be reproduced, stored in a retrieval system, or transmitted, in any form or by any means, electronic, mechanical, photocopying, recording, or otherwise, without the written permission of the author.

First published by Dog Ear Publishing
4010 W. 86th Street, Ste H
Indianapolis, IN 46268
www.dogearpublishing.net

ISBN: 978-160844-936-1

This book is printed on acid-free paper.

Printed in the United States of America

This book is dedicated to my family—to my sons, Mike, Brian, and Greg, and my lovely daughter Erin, who have heard these stories many times; to my gracious and understanding wife, Betty, who stood by me when the experiences of Vietnam made my life meaningless. But most importantly, this book is dedicated to the men and the families of the men who were killed and wounded in the defense of Khe Sanh Combat Base and the surrounding hills.

FOREWORD

The Moving Trees: Diary of a Khe Sanh Marine is a daily account carefully documented by a twenty-year-old marine who shares the taste, smells, sounds, sights, and feelings of the battlefields in Vietnam.

Written with the simplicity and honesty of a man facing death, it will cause you to chuckle at the mishaps and cry over the sorrows served up by war.

You will lounge with men whiling away boring hours and days, walk with them "through the wire" and on the sweeps through forbidding grasses and brush, crouch beside them in the heat of battle, and lie awake in the blackness of night, waiting to set off an ambush.

If you are curious enough to walk beside this young Marine, you will learn what it is to daily serve your country in a hostile environment. If you are brave enough, you will go up against the gooks while your comrades in Delta Company fall in battle on every side.

This is a daily account commencing on November 15, 1967, and concluding May 29, 1968, of a farm boy from West Virginia who is charged with the responsibility of keeping his men awake at their posts at night and, at length, commands men in the heat of battle when the officers are wounded or killed. You will hear his hot words of command, feel his tenderness toward the wounded and frightened, and hear him sob over the loss of his friends. The solemn strictures given to him by officers back in the world—"You don't make friends in combat. You just make acquaintances."—somehow seem harsh and irrelevant as his tears fall upon the faces of his "acquaintances" who were also his "friends."

As you walk beside this highly disciplined Marine, hear him chide his men for not wearing their helmets or falling asleep on watch, you will hear a change in his vocabulary and see a metamorphosis in his attitude toward the value of life and the business of war. A young man whose greatest concern at first was the sorrow that his beloved mother would feel if he died at length becomes steeled so he can say to a fellow Marine that he doesn't care any longer if he gets hit: "If I got hit and didn't die I'd be in a nice dry hospital bed tonight. If I got hit and died I'd probably be in Hell tonight and wouldn't care."

The war changed the young Marine. He came to hate the war, the gooks, and all that moved on the face of the earth out there where death awaited him:

I came to this bunker. I saw someone jump down into it as we were coming through the ville. I pulled the pin and threw a grenade down the hole, and it went off. I heard some yelling and screaming. So I just threw another one down there. I knew there were women and children down there, but I didn't care. I am tired of seeing people killed—my friends killed. These damn gooks—all I can think about is killing them. I am just tired of this place...

Deschaine's squad found some ammo. So we went back and burned the whole damn ville down. We killed their pigs and chickens, and anything that moved, we shot. If any gooks had come out of their holes, I would have loved to have killed them too...They all deserved to die.

'...I am tired of this war altogether. If anybody messes with me tonight, they are dead.'

Charles D. Mosher

PREFACE

This book covers the life of one infantry Marine from the time he leaves the United States on 14 November 1967 until his return on 30 May 1968. This account involves only those Marines who served with him. The Marine knows very little about what's going on in the next trench line, let alone what is going on in Saigon or back in the States.

Each day, the author of this book wrote something in his diary, and this book sprang forth from those notes. Khe Sanh was one of the major battles of the Vietnam War. In this book, the author shows not only what war is like but also, and more importantly, how war affects a young Marine.

As a member of the 1st Fire Team, 1st Squad, 1st Platoon, Delta Company, 1st Battalion 26th Marine Regiment, 1st Marine Division, this Marine transforms from an innocent young farm boy to a war-hardened platoon sergeant. His home is his bunker, and his family is his platoon. Killing becomes exciting and very easy to do. The only important thing in his life is staying alive and keeping the guys in his platoon alive.

The names in this book are the real names of the men who served with the author. The author wrote down the names and service numbers of all the men in his platoon while he was in Vietnam. Although he was unable to find the full names of everyone he came into contact with, rather than leave the names of those men out, he used the names as he had written them in his own diary.

There is a glossary of terms in the back of book.

This book is a true historical perspective of the battle for Khe Sanh during this time frame. It is based solely on the author's diary entries and his recollections. All the pictures were taken at Khe Sanh Combat Base, in the surrounding hills, and Delta Company's area of operations.

ACKNOWLEDGMENTS

I am very grateful to many individuals for the help and encouragement they gave me in the writing and editing of this book:

Doug Corbett, the only Marine I served with in Vietnam with whom I have had contact since we returned to the States. Our Christmas Eve phone conversations gave me the strength to write this book.

My wife Betty; sons, Mike, Brian, and Greg; and daughter, Erin.

Charles and Ruth Mosher, friends and authors in their right.

My parents, Bill and Regina Oyster.

November 15

Because I crossed the International Date Line, I lost this day. I will get it back on the return trip. I hope I'm sitting up.

November 16

We pulled out of El Toro Marine Air Station at 0800 on 14 November and landed here in Okinawa at 0130 today.

It was really neat. I knew my brother Bill (Bood, as we called him) was due to come home soon. As I was marching the formation up to the front of the air terminal at El Toro I kept looking for someone that might be on their way home from Vietnam. Just before we made a turn in the road I saw a Marine in winter greens standing in front of the door. When we got around the turn, I couldn't believe my eyes: there was Bood. I let the other guys take the troops on into the plane so I could visit with him. When I came up to him I gave him a big hug, picked him up and spun him around. He looked surprised to see me, but more surprised that I hugged him. That was the first time I had ever hugged him I think. We had a very bitter sweet reunion. He was happy to be heading home and I was scared—heading for Nam. We talked about the farm, and Mom and Dad. I told him everything seemed fine when I left. I asked him to tell Mom and Dad the same story I had told them—that I wouldn't be in the front lines, but in the rear with a Red-Eye missile platoon. I don't think Dad really believed me but I didn't want them to worry if I could help it.

I wanted him to tell me all he could about Vietnam. He had been stationed with the 235th VMF All-weather Fighter Squadron in Da-Nang. He said he had been under mortar and rocket attacks a few times but he never had to go out into the bush. He said he had talked to some guys who had been in the bush and they said it wasn't too bad. I think he said that for my benefit. I didn't know to what part of Vietnam I'd be sent, but Bood said the worst places were up north. He said he had heard the NVA were tough. They were well disciplined and well organized.

We both had to get going so we said our good-byes. Bood told me what seat he had sat in on the flight from Okinawa, and I sat in the same one going to Okinawa. He said he would keep me in his prayers. That scared me even more.

The plane flight was OK, but it was really long. We played acey-deucey on the plane and I won a little more than ten bucks. We landed in Hawaii and were on the ground for about three hours. The only thing I saw was the inside of the airport bar. The bartender pointed out what he said was Diamond Head way off in the distance, but I really didn't care. When we got back on the plane in Hawaii I took a head count and jumped on a couple of troops for being a little too hard on the stewardess. She came up to my seat a little later and asked me if I was a lifer and rubbed her nose against mine. I would have liked to have spent some time with her, but I knew that was never going to happen. All the girls tried to be friendly, but they knew that many of these young guys would never make it back home alive. I wanted to talk to one of them about how they felt about their job, but I couldn't, because I may be one of those guys who don't make it home.

As I looked around at the young men on the plane, I wondered who would be killed and who would survive. Would I make it? I made up my mind right then and there that I wouldn't let myself think about dying again. I would do my best, do what I was told to do, try not to do anything stupid, and pray to God I'd make it home in one piece. It's kind of funny—as I thought about dying, I didn't think about what it would be like to be dead but how much it would hurt my mother if I got killed.

As I was thinking about Mom, I couldn't help reminiscing over my twenty years of life. Growing up on a small farm in West Virginia, the oldest boy in our family of seven kids, I learned to work at an early age. My older sister Mary and I were close, but we were all close. Mom and Dad raised us tough. Discipline was a major part of our life. I think their discipline has helped me so far in the Corps. Playing football, baseball, wrestling, running track, and always thinking I was cool with the girls was how I grew up.

I joined the Marine Corps because the Army and the Navy recruiters were not in the day I made up my mind to go into the service. I went to the post office in East Liverpool, Ohio, to join the Army on July 20, 1964. I had gone there with a buddy of mine from high school and we were going to join the Army on the buddy plan. I waited for over an hour for the recruiter, and when he didn't show up I walked over to the city hall building to join the Navy. I looked in his office, and he wasn't there either. As I was coming down the hall, the Marine Corps recruiter yelled out that he could help me, and that's how I ended up in the Marine Corps. I didn't want to join the Corps, because my uncle Hank Tabor had been killed in WW II and he had been a Marine. I grew up thinking all Marines get killed in war.

I made PFC out of basic training and really thought I was tough. I then went on to ITR at Camp Lejeune, North Carolina, and real Marine training. I really enjoyed infantry training, because that's what Marines are supposed to do. I spent two years as a security guard aboard ship and got to travel around Europe. I got busted the second year aboard ship, a six month suspended bust for calling a sailor I was guarding in the brig a dumb son of a bitch. Then they took my corporal stripe for getting into it with another Marine in our detachment. When I came back to the States I went to a redeye missile platoon at Camp Lejeune, North Carolina. It was really boring. I volunteered for Vietnam when I found out my younger brother Bood was going. I couldn't let him outdo me. It took almost a year for all the paperwork to go through. I had to sign a waiver because Bood was already there. (Our government didn't want two brothers in country at the same time).

I'm on my way to war now and I hope all the discipline and love my family has given me will help me make it home again.

When we got off the plane in Okinawa we were loaded into cattle cars and brought to Camp Butler. They gave us all a rack and I went to sleep. Got up at 0930, stood around in a couple of formations, not much to do here. I was hoping I could get off the base. I wanted to see if I could find out where my Uncle

Hank had been killed. I went to CO Headquarters and they said no. No one was allowed to leave the base. They were afraid if you left you wouldn't come back.

I went down to the EM club, had a few beers, and bitched with the rest of the guys. Everyone hopes we'll get out of here tomorrow.

November 17

Well, I'm now on the plane for Vietnam.

They got us up about 0800 hours, and we went out and stood in formation while this gunnery sergeant talked to us about what we were supposed to do, what to expect, and so forth. We had to separate all our gear. We left one sea bag there. He told us we needed no dress uniforms. So everybody cleared out their stuff, loaded it on cattle cars and a couple trucks, and took them over to this great huge building. There must have been three million sea bags in there. As I looked at all those sea bags my mind began to race. Who are all these guys, where are all these guys, are they alive, are they wounded, are they dead? We took our sea bags into the building and just stacked them up. They said when we leave Vietnam, we will come back through Okinawa and they'll process us through again and we'll pick up our sea bags. It was sort of strange; it was as if it were a beginning/ending process. We were leaving the only life we had known and going into something that will be really strange and kind of frightening. And I am sitting here on this plane thinking, what am I getting into?

After we got our sea bags stored, they let us just hang around for the rest of the day, but we had to be ready to go by 2200 hours. So we headed over to the club about 1600 and had a couple of beers and just waited. The conversations were a lot like the ones we had on the bus from Savannah to Parris Island as we headed into basic training. People talk and no one really listens. We are all lost in our own thoughts. Everyone is wondering what it's going to be like, will I get along OK, and, most importantly, will I make it back to the world?

At 2100 hours we headed over to the tarmac and got on the plane. It scares me, but when this plane lands we'll really be in Vietnam and into the war.

November 18

Staying at 1/26 rear, Phu Bai, South Vietnam

It's the end of my first day in beautiful Vietnam. We left Okinawa at 2345 and got into Da Nang at 0730. It was really strange. I don't know what I really expected, I guess dirt and mud and something that looked like war. But when we landed it looked like we were landing at the Pittsburgh Airport. There were all kinds of trucks and buses and cars, and all kinds of machines and people loading and unloading luggage. One thing I did believe though, it's hot—-even at 0730 it's hot.

After we got off the plane, they herded us to a building, and of course everybody was nervous, carrying their equipment and didn't know what to do. Most of us had the feeling that we were going to get shot at any moment. It's really pretty peaceful here; not much going on around Da Nang anyway. After they talked to us for a while, they handed out orders, and I found that I was going to a place called Khe Sanh with the 1st Battalion 26th Marines. I asked around, and no one seemed to know where Khe Sanh is except that it's somewhere in the northern I-Corp. The unique thing about this place is that you've got to find your own transportation. It's not like I expected. I was sure they'd have some means of transportation lined up for us. They told me that I had to head for Phu Bai, which was a base north of Da Nang but not quite as far north as Khe Sanh. So Heath [James G., 2109322] and I headed for a helicopter pad and talked to a couple guys about a ride north. They said they had a helicopter going up to Phu Bai and we could get aboard. We got into Phu Bai at 1430. Heath and I have been stationed together before, and it is nice to come into country with someone you know. He made sergeant while we were at Pendleton. I made it back to corporal; I would have made sergeant if I hadn't gotten busted back on the *USS Canopus*. I think I got screwed, but maybe I'd be better off if I'd learn to keep my mouth shut.

We're staying at 1/26 rear and they said they'd get us up to Khe Sanh as quickly as they could. No one seems to know of anything going out anytime soon. Not much to do; we just sit around and wait near the helicopter pad hoping somebody will give us a ride to Khe Sanh. We asked if we could have a place to sleep tonight; we want to stay as near the helicopter pad as we can. They said yeah and they put us over here in the TAD (temporary additional duty) barracks. This is a place to wait and sleep. This place is a lot different than I expected. I really thought I'd find North Vietnamese running around all over the place and we'd be having trouble, but it is nothing like that at all. So for my first night in Vietnam I'm going to be sleeping in a barracks, nice and quiet just like it was back in the States.

November 19

We got our first taste of war at about 0200 this morning. Right outside our hooch, a 175 mm howitzer blasted off a few rounds, and it scared the living hell out of me. I jumped up and ran out of the hooch to see what was going on, which was a dumb thing to do in the first place. I probably just should have stayed right where I was rather than taking a chance and getting outside and getting shot. But I had no idea what it was. I went outside, and there were these guys firing off this 175 and it made a tremendous amount of noise and really scared me, so I guess this is really my first taste of war.

Heath and I just hung around here all day and tried to find out a little bit more about Khe Sanh and the 1/26 Marines. Thought we had a ride up to Khe Sanh; the chopper was leaving but we were the last people to get in line and didn't get on, so we will just have to wait another day. We went over to the club; they have a little club here—-really nothing but a little hooch where they sell beer. We had a few beers and got to talk to some of the guys. Didn't know anybody or didn't get to know anybody too well, but it was an interesting night.

Phu Bai looks like what I expected Vietnam to look like, the hooches and the mud and so forth. It is not completely what I expected but I think it's a little more along the lines of what I thought war is supposed to look like.

We had another eye opener today. We were sitting over by the runway when these two choppers came in. I wasn't real close but it looked like they were bringing in dead Marines in body bags. I wanted to know where they were coming from but I didn't ask. I hope it wasn't Khe Sanh. Of course I didn't know any of them, but it still made me half sick. I'm sure I'll never get used to all this death.

I hope I can get some sleep tonight; maybe we'll get out of here tomorrow.

November 20

I finally made it to Khe Sanh. We got a ride out of Phu Bai at 0930 today. While we were flying over Khe Sanh I thought, boy this is just like West Virginia; it is beautiful country and lots of trees and greenery. It is really beautiful. Khe Sanh Combat Base is about a mile long and a half mile wide. It has a runway made of metal matting along the east side and tents and a trench line to the west. Khe Sanh Village is about three miles to the southwest.

We flew up here in a Caribou and you could look out the windows and they had the back open too so you could see out the back. It looks like the grass is short, but I found out when I talked to some of the guys here its 12-foot-high elephant grass.

It is pretty peaceful around here. It is not really much like war, but it looks more like what I have seen in pictures of World

War II, the mud and so forth. Both Heath and I are going to Delta Company. We have to have four days of classes before we can go out to our platoon. We are sleeping in a CP tent on cots. There is no electricity, but it's not too bad I guess. A little more like what I expected war to look like. It's really pretty peaceful around here; the guys don't even wear helmets. They just walk around in their shirts. The discipline looks OK. It doesn't seem like anybody really puts the pressure on you like they do in the States.

I should find out more about this place tomorrow. I should be able to sleep OK tonight, pretty quiet right now.

November 21

I sure didn't get much sleep last night. They have 155 and 105 mm howitzers here and they fire H and I every night. I really don't know what the story is, I don't think it is anything going on around us, but they fire those things out every night. I don't think I will ever get used to it. The noise of them going off wakes me up every time. We are just living in this tent, so you can hear everything. There is no insulation or anything to protect you from the sound, so boy when they fire, I jump. The guys say I will get used to it eventually, but I am not sure that I ever will. This place is really kind of neat. They roll you out about 0800 and you have a choice. If you want to go to chow, you can, they have a chow hall and really have pretty good chow; if you don't want chow, you don't have to go. They say that every Sunday morning they have a really great breakfast. So I am looking forward to that. The hot chow is pretty nice. You have to use your mess kit and they have big barrels to wash them out like we did back in basic training. It's funny, I haven't seen one of those things in a long time.

We had our first day of classes today. The classes aren't too tough, just kind of an indoctrination into what's going on around here and what they expect you to do.

I met a guy named Deschaine [Norman C., 2131988] today. He's from South Chicago and he is alright, I guess. He thinks he knows everything. He's a corporal and it's funny because no matter what the staff sergeant was talking about, he already knew it. He is kind of arrogant, but I guess we can get along. We will probably end up in the same platoon so I'd better be able to get along with him. I found out something today that put the fear of God into me. This is where Hill 881 is; they had a whale of a battle up there in May. I had no idea I was going to end up here. There were all kinds of Marines killed on Hill 881. This place is a lot more dangerous than I expected it to be. We also man Hills 861 and 950. There is a company up on Hill 881 and Hill 861 right now and they have a platoon on 950, which is just a pinhead of a hill in the range east of here. You can see it from here; it's really high and small. There is really not much area to cover, and not much area for protection. I hope I don't get sent up there. They said we will be on 861, and they have been getting attacked occasionally. So it looks like I am going to finally get my first taste of war.

I'm sleeping or at least lying down in this tent again tonight. Maybe they won't fire all night and I'll get some sleep.

November 22

We had our second day of class today, and like I said, it wasn't too tough. They just talk to you about what is going on around here and what they expect out of you at the base, but they haven't had any action here since July. There hasn't been a bullet fired in anger, so that is kind of good. Maybe I really lucked out and this place really won't be too bad.

It is really beautiful country. It reminds me of the mountains of West Virginia: a lot of hills and ups and downs. The guys say when you are out humping it is really tough terrain to get through. I don't know anything about the jungle, but it is beautiful; you look out across those hills when the sun is shining and it's just really gorgeous. I'm sure I'm going to enjoy getting out there and jumping around those hills. It will be just like being back on the farm.

I asked some of the guys if they have an EM club or if they get any beer and they said no, they didn't. There is no club of any kind here. We do have a chaplain that has mass on Sundays, so at least I will get to go to mass. Being a good Irish Catholic, I should do that.

I guess it's been real peaceful around here. It is just like being back at a base like Da Nang or back in the States even. Not much going on. We do run a few patrols outside the base. We go out around the wire, check it for breaks and do work details. There is really not too much happening right now which is just fine with me.

I slept better last night—maybe I'll really sleep tonight.

November 23

This is our third day of classes. I am going to be glad when this stuff is over. They are not really telling us a whole lot of new information or anything that I can really use. It is just time spent, I guess. They did tell us today that we have four companies in 1/26. We have two artillery batteries which have been firing these 155s and 105s every night. The way the companies are set up, we have one company, Bravo Company, which is on Hill 881. We have Charlie Company on 861 and a platoon from someplace—I don't know, they really didn't say what company it was from—on Hill 950. The company on the line, which is I guess where the platoon came from, is Alpha. A company in the rear for operations, that's Delta Company, that's the company that I will be in. They are out on patrol now. They didn't say where they went, but they said they would be in tomorrow, so I am looking forward to that. They call it a reserve company, but they are the ones that do all the work I guess. Everybody else mans the lines or mans a position and then this company goes out and does all the patrols. They said they rotated some so I won't be on patrol all the time. I will spend some time on the lines, on Hill 881 and Hill 861, but I am really hoping I don't get sent up to Hill 950.

I look up at that hill and see there's just a pin sticking up and it is real steep on all four sides. I don't know how they can control it. It would be really frightening to be up there and have to defend something that small. I can't see why the North Vietnamese would even hesitate to overrun the place, with only a platoon up there. I mean, you figure a platoon is what, 40 guys. That's not very many guys to hold the top of that hill. It is not a very big hill, so I bet one platoon can encircle the whole place. I don't want to find out. Man, I hope I don't get sent up there.

I'm still in the tent but not sleeping real well.

November 24

I finally got through the last day of classes and didn't really learn a lot, I guess, or it didn't seem like I did.

The company came in early this afternoon and I met some of the guys! One fellow is from Youngstown, named Wilson, [Warren A., 2294472]. Seemed like a pretty good bunch of guys. I am going to 1st Platoon and Heath is going to 2nd. It's kind of strange; we have been together for a long time, you know, aboard the ship and everything else, and here we are, still in the same company. We are in different platoons but I will get to see him once in a while. Like every place else I've been stationed, I will meet some new guys and make some new friends, although you don't make friends—I found out you make military acquaintances in combat. This is one of the things they told us in our classes: make friends, be friends with the guys, but don't get so attached to somebody that it is going to affect you when they get killed. Chances are in a combat situation, a lot of people will get killed or wounded and you won't see them again. I never thought about that before. I guess they are right—if Heath got blown away, it would hurt me.

I'm starting to get used to the guns. I didn't think I ever would, but I slept pretty well last night. It's like anything else, I guess—the more you are around it, the more you get used to it.

I'm hoping that I get out to my platoon tomorrow. 1st Platoon is in the rear, so they are sleeping in tents over in the company area. It will be about the same as this but a little farther away from the guns.

November 25

It's neat—get up at 0800, or whenever you feel like it, and go to chow if you want to. It's really strange, it is not at all what I expected. I knew it would be different than in the States. I guess I expected to be shooting at someone every day.

They took us over to our platoons early this morning. I am in 1st Platoon. I got a bunk in the tent with the rest of the guys in my squad. Didn't do much today; just kind of fooled around the area and talked to some of the guys. I was told all the new guys have a meeting at 1730 with the company commander, Lt. Spencer, [Ernest E., 092222]. He is going to talk to us a little while and then we are going to meet with our platoon commanders. My platoon commander is Second Lt. Sharples [Charles, 0102273]. I talked to some of the guys around here, and they said both officers are pretty good leaders.

While Lt. Spencer was talking to us, we got the word that 2nd platoon was pulling out on a sparrow hawk, and Heath said he was going with them. I don't know if he did or not. I haven't seen him since, so I guess maybe he did. Wouldn't you know it he gets to be the first one of us to hit the bush. I'm going to be in the 1st Squad. I haven't met the squad leader yet—Angle, Gale (service number not available)—but the guys tell me he's good. All the guys I have met seem like a good bunch of guys.

Some of these troops have been here for a year, and it shows. I am the young hard-nose, ready-to-go, full-of-excitement kid, and some of the other new guys are too. Some of the older men are younger than I am in age but they seem much older. The signs of war have worn a pretty deep scar on some of them—you can tell it when you talk to them. But you never know; it seems like they don't really develop that closeness that I thought would be there. They are lonely, almost; it is a strange feeling to see these guys and talk to them and they will share things and talk to you but they never really get into that in-depth conversation when you really get to know them. I suppose I understand that because we will go out on patrol one of these days and I'll be walking along beside somebody and he'll get killed or maybe I'll get killed and that friendship is something that can really tear into you. I want to make friends with these guys, and I need their support and they need mine. We have got to depend on each other, but I don't know how I am going to handle it the first time I see one of these guys get killed or, God forbid, I get killed. I sure don't want that to happen to me. It would be just too much for my mom to take. I don't know, I guess I will just try to play it by ear and try to do what everybody else does.

It is funny to look for reasons to stay alive and my basic reason is my mother. I know she loves me very much and I love her and that if something happened to me it would be devastating to her, and I don't want to die. I want to live; I have a lot of things I want to do with my life, but when I think about how it would affect Mom, I want to be more and more careful. I can just see her getting a message, or telegram, or however they tell parents back home that their son has been killed. It would be awful for her; I don't know if she could even get over it—if she would ever get over it. So I just pray to God that nothing happens to me and she never has to go through that. I think about Mom, and Dad too of course, but mainly Mom. When I was growing up she was the one who was always there for me. She beat my butt when I needed it and was the first one to pat me on the back when I did something good. So Mom, for you, I'm going to bring my butt back to the world in one piece.

I got a new tent and new cot. Maybe I'll sleep great tonight.

November 26

I like this place more and more. They wake you up if you want to go to chow, and if you don't, they don't even wake you up. We have to be showered, and they have a police call around the area by 0900. That's really all we have to do. Some days it's fun to get up for chow. And some days it's not, so you sleep in or do whatever you want. I'm not big on getting up in the morning.

We went out on a sparrow hawk today. Went out about 3 clicks and set in for a little while and then came back. Just kind of checked out the area, didn't really have too much to do, just walk around. It's a lot tougher than I thought. The hills are a lot steeper than they look. If you stay on the trails you can move pretty fast, but if you get off them it's really tough going. When we came back in, Lt. Sharples, our platoon commander, talked to me about taking some classes, so I'm going to have to take those MCI classes. Lt. Sharples got hit by a water buffalo when he was out on the last operation. He didn't get hurt bad, just stoved-up, but he can't go out if something happens. So like today and anytime we have to go out for the next few weeks, some other officer will have to go with us.

The sparrow hawk really surprised me; I thought we would be walking through the underbrush. We actually walked on trails and didn't have to cut too much underbrush or anything, so it really wasn't too hard. It was sort of like a stroll through a park but the heat made it rough going. It's hot and damp, so it's really not too much fun. Your clothes are wet as soon as you get started. One of the things they told us in class was to drink lots of water. Now I know why. The only clothes you wear are boots, pants, and your shirt. No one wears socks or underwear. First of all, you don't need them, and you really don't have a good place to wash them.

Another day is over and I'm still alive.

November 27

I found out what kind of person we have for an XO when we got called out today. We were sitting there having a class and just visiting and talking and fooling around. When we got the word to saddle up we went over to the LZ, and loaded on CH 34s. They took us out to Hill 420. I couldn't believe it, the chopper was still six to eight feet off the ground when they told us to get out. I jumped out, landed on my feet in that ten-foot-high elephant grass everyone has been talking about. We made plans to meet just off the LZ. Getting through that grass was something. I now know how an ant feels. We did get everyone together OK and moved off the LZ. We just walked around the base of the hill and up over the side. It was pretty rough going. The hill wasn't too steep but the grass was tough to get through. We got the word to set in and they were going to drop chow in to us. I don't know why we didn't bring anything with us to eat, but they did get chow in to us.

I'm not a great military mind, but where the XO set us in scared the hell out of me. He set us in at the base of this hill. Everything I have been taught about combat procedures told me we would be safer up closer to the top of the hill. I've not been in country very long, but where we were seemed crazy to me. If the gooks got up on the hill above our position they could roll grenades down on us. The guys who had been here a long time weren't too happy either. He could at least put us in near the top of the ridge. Where we're sitting, the gooks can come up the other side and just wipe our whole platoon out. I'm not sure the XO knows what he's doing, but again he's the XO. You've got to do what he tells you. I don't think anybody will frag him or anything but we'll just have to wait and see. I'm not going to get much sleep tonight. This is not a good place to be. We're right here on the edge of this finger, so we have no protection. If the gooks come up the other side of the hill we'll really be in trouble.

I sat in with a guy everyone calls Shortround [McCulley, Floyd A., 8326683]. He is a really good guy. We talked about our families and what we will do when we get back to the world.

This is not a safe place, but I have to get some sleep.

November 28

November 28 was pretty uneventful. They didn't hit us last night, thank God. When we got up we just patrolled the area, we went a couple clicks, then headed back in toward the base, so it really wasn't very exciting. I was really nervous though; I guess the first time you're in the field you get that way. I mean you get used to it eventually, but the first time you are in the field it really bothers you. I kept thinking that we could walk into an ambush. Although there weren't a lot of trees and stuff where the gooks could set one up, I couldn't stop thinking about it. There was just grass until we got down into the valley less than a click from the base. Then there were some trees and bushes. I guess I'll get used to it after a while, but staying on the trails and walking in columns, I just think we were setting ourselves up for an ambush. It wouldn't take much at all for gooks to set up along the edge of the trail and just wipe us out.

We got back in here about 1430 and had some chow. Things are pretty quiet around here. We get all kinds of scuttlebutt. People are continually telling all kinds of stories about what's going on, what is going to happen to us, and everything else you can think of. They told us today that it looks like we are going to 881 tomorrow and take over for whoever is up there. Our platoon will be going up along with some reinforcements. We will have some machine guns and I don't know what else, but that's what the word is. We are going to 881 in the morning, so I'll sleep well here tonight in my little cot and we'll see where I am tomorrow. I am really nervous about going up on the hills. I have heard so much about them and read so much about the attacks and fighting that went on up there. The guys say it is not too bad, so we'll just have to go up there and see. The way stories get told around here, we may end up in Da Nang.

November 29

I spent my first day on the hill, and it is more like what I thought war was going to be like. They rolled us out at 0700, we had chow, loaded on Hueys, and up we came.

This place is disgusting. It has been raining for four days and the bunkers are all washed out. There is really no protection. I mean, the bunkers we're in are about safe enough to stop a bullet from an AK-47, but that's about it. Just mud everywhere; it's really awful, and I don't know how long we are going to be up here. They told us the first thing we have to do is try to reinforce these bunkers. We have to dig down a little deeper to make them a little safer. The trench line around the outside is not bad, but it's not very deep. It is only about four feet deep, but at least you can get down out of the line of fire. We are right on top of the hill and with one finger going out to the edge. It's pretty much the peak of the hill. If we can get this place shored up a little bit and make our bunkers a little better, maybe, it won't be so bad.

No hot chow up here. We are eating C-rations, which aren't too bad. I can eat those beans and weenies, but ham and lima beans are my favorite. No one likes ham and lima beans, so everyone gives them to me. So I eat good.

I'm scared here on this hill but I think everybody else is too, except maybe the old salts. Some of the old guys don't seem too upset about it, at least at this point. We'll see what happens. One of the major battles of the war has been fought up here. Let's hope that they don't have any more. We had to send out the listening posts tonight. I didn't know if they would send me out on one or not. Right now I am sort of the oddball, being a corporal and a fire team leader, but I found out at 1600 I was going out at 2100. I didn't mind going out once just to see what it was like. This way when I send someone out, I'll have some idea what it's like. It was really scary on the way out, and when we first set in, just sitting there doing nothing, thinking about all the men that were killed on this hill last May when they had the big attack. They overran the hill. They overran 881. It was scary, but it was exciting. I went out with Corbett [Douglas S., 2357151]. I think we could become good friends. It wasn't too bad after a while. We talked a little but not much, just looked out into the darkness. One of the old guys told me to watch out for the moving trees. I thought he was nuts, but now I know what he was talking about. After we had been sitting there for a couple of hours and staring at the trees I swear they moved. At first I thought it was a man, then I realized it was just my mind playing tricks on me. They brought us in right before daylight. All in all, it wasn't too bad.

One good thing about being on LP, you can sleep while everyone else is working. I hope I can get some sleep.

November 30

I spent the day working on the bunkers, trench line, and fighting holes. The rain has really washed things out. Even though it stopped raining for a little while today, it has still rained most of the day. This red clay is so slick, you start up the hill and you just slide all over the place. It's worse than being on ice.

We had some mail flown in today. It's the first mail I have received since I have been here. I received two letters from Mom. It was really nice to hear from the people back home. Also, I was really glad to see that everyone got something. I know all of the guys in my platoon received something in the mail. There were some packages; Huskey [John, 2317625] got a box of cookies and passed them around. So everybody had a little something.

I went out on a listening post again tonight. I went out with Parker [David A., 2283592]. They took us out about 2030. We had to crawl through the wire this time. It was my second time out so I felt a little better than the first time. We went out about a hundred yards outside the wire. There were some trees there so we sat up against them. It was so dark! You just can't believe how dark it was. The only way I can describe it to anybody would be for you to get into a closet and shut the door. Have all the lights off in the room, and that might give you some idea of how dark it is. Once we got set in I was a little nervous but then I settled down. You just sit there and do what you are told. You listen; you have the radio with you, and the squelch is turned on so you just key the hand set. If you hear something you start keying the handset real fast, and whoever is on watch inside the base will start talking to you. You answer their questions by keying the hand set once for yes and twice for no. We sat out there for about six hours and didn't see a thing. I was really glad to get back inside but less nervous than last night.

Second listening post over, got some mail, good day.

December 1

I slept pretty well last night. We worked on our bunkers most of the day. The bunkers are in real bad shape. The rain has washed them out some. Whoever was here before us didn't take very good care of them.

Our squad had an ambush tonight. I was really scared when we were going out. I was sure we'd walk into a bunch of gooks. Once we got set in, I settled down a little. We stopped along the trail and just stepped off it and sat down. We were about six feet off the trail and facing it. We sat there for four hours and didn't see or hear anything. I was sitting about in the middle of the line of troops. I had no trouble staying awake, but some of the guys went to sleep. I don't know how they did it.

We came in about 0100. I'm going to sleep now.

December 2

I didn't get much sleep last night. I kept thinking what could have happened on that ambush. I guess God was on my side.

It didn't rain at all today. The weather was nice.

I didn't do much but work on the bunkers today. I'm going out on a patrol tomorrow. I'm not looking forward to that. It's really strange, all the feelings you have about this place. I didn't want to come up here in the first place, and now that I'm up here I don't want to go outside the wire. I can't say I feel safe inside the wire but I feel safer than outside it. I know I have been trained to fight and maybe I should be excited about doing it but today I'm a scared little boy.

I don't feel much like sleeping, but I've got to.

December 3

I slept OK but not great. Huskey is in my bunker with me now, and that gives me someone to talk to.

Our squad went out on patrol today. We jumped off at 0830. We humped out about two clicks altogether. We went out through the wire on the north side of the hill. We just traveled along in columns, one guy behind the other. We went down the hill and off to the west. We walked on the trails most of the way. When we did get off the trail it was tough going. We circled around to the north and came back in at about 1400.

I was a little scared at first, but after a while I got used to it. Some of the old guys just walked along like they were on a Sunday stroll. They lit up a smoke whenever they wanted. I am not that brave yet.

I didn't have any watches, so I can go to sleep. I'm really tired.

December 4

I slept pretty well last night; I was tired. We didn't do much at all today. The word is we are going back down to Khe Sanh tomorrow. I wish they would put us someplace and leave us there. That way I wouldn't mind working so hard on the bunkers and trenches. It seems like we just get someplace liveable and we move.

We have one of our platoons up on Hill 950, and they got hit the other night. I heard the gooks were throwing grenades in on them and they fired some tank rounds back at them. No one knew if they killed any gooks.

I think I'll sleep better tonight just knowing we'll be off this hill tomorrow.

December 5

Up at 0530 and got my gear ready to go. Bravo Company came in through the wire at 1145. They have been out on patrol for three days. We pulled out at 1300 and headed out to the south. We picked up a trail and moved pretty fast for about an hour. We then left the trail and moved toward the east. It was hard cutting through the bush. We picked up some trail, but we still moved slowly. At about 1800 we got the word to set in for the night. We're someplace near Hill 600 according to the map. We are set in right near the top of this hill. I think Lt. Sharples knows what he is doing.

I'm getting so I can read the map pretty well. We are given thrust points to put on the map. We are using dogs at longitude 42, latitude 80; flowers at longitude 44, latitude 75; and rivers at longitude 45, latitude 79. What we do then is say north one half click from boxers, and east four and a half clicks from roses. The Gooks have the same maps, so it makes it easy for us, and they don't know where our thrust points are so they can't tell where we are.

I feel pretty good about where we are tonight—I'll sleep OK.

December 6

I didn't sleep very well. The LPs had some movement and everyone was up ready to fight if the gooks hit us. I was really scared. I knew what I had to do but, for a few minutes when I first woke up I couldn't stop shaking. Nothing happened so I toughened up. I wonder what I'll be like when something does happen.

We started out for Khe Sanh at 0800 and moved fairly fast. It wasn't as fast as we could go, but not too bad. We got back into the base at 1535.

We are back in our tents; I hope we stay here for a while.

We had hot chow and just hung around the area. I got in a card game with Huskey, Corbett, and Shortround. I lost my butt.

We left Hill 881 just in time. Bravo Co. took some small-arms fire yesterday and a chopper took some today trying to resupply them. It's nice to be back inside the wire of Khe Sanh. I'll sleep better tonight.

December 7

I slept real well last night. Up at 0800, had chow, did a police call and just hung out the rest of the day.

I was thinking to myself today. Wasn't December 7th the day the Japs bombed Pearl Harbor? I hope the gooks aren't going to use today as a good day to hit us.

We got the word we are going out on a patrol tomorrow. I guess we are going down Highway 9 to some plantation. Not too many of the guys have been down that way before, so nobody knows for sure what's down there.

I cleaned my rifle real good today. It's funny, when I was at Parris Island and we cleaned our rifles I never thought much about it. While I was cleaning it today, I thought, "I want this thing to fire every time I pull the trigger." I did it just like we were taught. I checked the recoil spring real close; from what I hear, it's the recoil spring in the M-16 that causes it not to fire. The gunny came around with a couple other staff NCOs and looked them over. I think everyone had their rifle cleaned. I guess when you are counting on it to protect you, you had better take better care of it.

I feel pretty good tonight. I should sleep well.

December 8

Up at 0600, had chow, and we were ready to pull out at 0800. We went out through the ARVN lines, and down Highway 9. It was an easy hump. We walked along like we didn't have anything to look for. We went through a wooded area where the trees had been planted but not taken care of for a while. Corbett said it was a rubber plantation that some French family had been running until the war came along. The house was still lived in but we didn't stop near it. I could see people around the house, but I couldn't tell if they were French. We were back inside the base at 1630.

Today was very strange. Seeing that plantation reminded me of pictures I had seen of World War II. The house looked like it was a very nice place before the war. The plantation probably had several Vietnamese working there. Maybe some of the Bru worked there. I thought we were here to help these people, but things like I saw today make me wonder if we are doing anyone any good being here.

I can't get that plantation out of my mind, but I'm hitting the rack and hope I can sleep.

December 9

Up at 0730 today, felt great. I don't know what made me feel so good, but I did. It was the best night's sleep I've had since I've been here.

I had to ride security on the truck making a run down to the dump. What a sight that was. When we got to the dump, the Bru were already waiting for us. They were a sad-looking lot. They were dressed in dirty old utilities with hats and boots. Some of their boots looked a little big. Just as soon as we dumped the stuff off the truck, they were into it, gathering up things they could use. They had little bags on their sides to put stuff into. I felt sorry for them at first, but they didn't seem at all unhappy. I guess if that is the way you have been living all your life, you think it's OK. I heard they are (or were) a nomadic tribe before the war. I wonder if the war hasn't changed that. I know with wild animals, like bears, once they start going to the human dumps they give up their normal way of gathering food.

The truck driver said they chew a root called beetle-nut all the time, that's why their teeth are so black. He also said they would trade us some if we wanted it. I didn't want any—I don't need black teeth.

I didn't do much the rest of the day. I'm hitting the rack at 2215.

December 10

I had a real problem getting up and going this morning. I took our squad over to the end of the runway to put out some tanglefoot wire. We didn't work too hard. Back over here at 1400 and didn't do a thing the rest of the day. I went to chow and back in the tent; now I'm ready to sack out.

December 11

Good day, received some mail from home. I got a letter from my brother Larry and a package from Mom. She sent me some cookies, which I shared with the guys like she told me to. I'm a good boy, Mom. She also sent me some things to remind me of Christmas. She sent me two candleholders that, when you turn them upside down, shake them, and turn them back over, it looks like it's snowing. Also a small Christmas tree already decorated. I got some other things from people I don't know, and I'm making a Christmas corner in my bunker.

Mom's letter had only good things to say about home. I hope she isn't keeping things from me she doesn't want me to know. My brother Larry's letter was greatest—he told me about school and all the things he is doing. I hope he doesn't join the service when he graduates.

December 12

I rolled out of the rack at 0800. It was nice to see my little Christmas corner. Even though I'm far from home I can have a little bit of home with me. I really don't know any of the guys well enough to talk about the things I think about, like Christmas and family, but it's nice to look at these things and think of home.

Intelligence says the gooks are building up around the base. They say a lot more gooks and gook material have been found. Each one of the hills has had some contact. Some of the patrols have had some also. We have had some air strikes on down the valley from us. I think some of the air strikes were B-52s. I haven't been here long enough to know for sure, but that's what somebody said.

We got the word to keep our helmets close at hand and we may start wearing our flak jackets. That thing is so uncomfortable and hot.

Hill 950 got hit again. I don't know who is up there, but I'm glad it's not me. All of Delta Company is inside the base.

Getting pretty boring around here. No, I don't think it's boring, I think I'm just getting used to it. At least I can sleep OK.

December 13

Up at 0800, went to chow. I had to go on a work detail over to Gray Alpha Sector today. I didn't have to do much since I'm a corporal. We filled sandbags all day. We filled them and put them on the trench line.

Intelligence says that we are going to get hit soon. I don't like being in this makeshift bunker if they do hit us.

3rd Battalion 26th Marines started flying in today. They are going to set in out toward Khe Sanh Ville. There isn't any real tall grass or big trees out there. If they get some holes dug right away, they should be OK.

Not too much to say about today—maybe I'll have more tomorrow.

December 14

I was up at 0800, had chow. Out on work party all day, just about the same as yesterday.

We got the word we're going back up to Hill 861. I don't know how much I'm going to like it, but getting out of here for a while can't be all bad. It's really funny—just a few days ago, I couldn't wait to get back inside the wire of Khe Sanh. Maybe I'm starting to "get tough." All the hills have been getting some action. Not a lot on 861, but 950 and 881 have had the most.

The skipper told us to get all the gear we have ready to move. It looks like we will be up there for a while. He said to be on the runway ready to move out at 0900.

I put my Christmas stuff in my seabag—I won't be taking it up with me. This will be the shortest Christmas season I've ever had.

We have been on the base about two weeks now. I have seen some things that look like war, the Bru at the dump, the plantation, and all the gook buildup. Before I'm back here again, I may see some combat.

December 15

Up at 0745, had chow and headed over to the airstrip. We were ready to move out at 0900 but didn't get started until 0945. We were loaded on CH-46s and ferried up to Hill 861. It was pretty uneventful. We off-loaded and made our way back to the bunkers we had before when we were up here. I'm sharing a bunker with Bob Green [Robert J., 2341663] and a couple other guys.

We spent most of the day off-loading our gear and getting everything set up. We had to help get the Co. gear carried from the landing pad to the command bunker. We brought up just about everything the company has; that's a good sign, maybe we are going to stay here for a while.

The bunker we're staying in is better than it was when we left. Someone put more sandbags around it. We still want to do some more with it. I would like to put another row of sandbags on top, and at least one more row around the sides. I can't believe how much time and energy we spend talking and working on our bunkers. I guess if I were back in the world, living on a nice quiet street, I would spend the same amount of time on my house. These bunkers are our homes.

My platoon had to send out the listening posts, but I didn't have to go. I don't know who went out; they weren't from my squad.

I'm glad we're off the base—it was getting boring down there. When we get bored, we get careless. I don't want to get careless, and I don't want the guys around me to get careless either.

I have only been out of the States a month, but it seems like a lot longer. Some of the old guys say you start to change the first day you're here. I don't think I've changed that much, but I am looking at things differently.

This looks like it's going to be my home for a while. We will make this bunker the best one on the hill.

December 16

I didn't get up until after 0800 this morning. No one woke me, and no one was looking for me. Just hung around the area today working on our bunker.

We heard Charlie Company got some action out east of Khe Sanh yesterday. I don't know if it's true or not. We did see some choppers out that way yesterday, but it looked like they were resupplying someone.

LPs had some movement last night. The line fired some jack-offs but didn't see anything. The LPs probably saw those moving trees.

My squad has a patrol tomorrow. We are going out toward Hill 881 North. They told us to take our packs, plenty of ammunition, and enough C-rations for a couple days.

I hope I sleep well tonight. It may be a few days before I sleep well again.

December 17

I rolled out of the rack at 0630. I ate some ham and lima beans for breakfast, my favorite. I was ready to motor at 0700, but we didn't go then. It was really foggy. I don't think I have ever seen fog that thick. The gooks could have walked right up to the wire before we would have seen them. They put everyone on the lines. We were on the lines until about 1100. It was kind of nice just sitting there shooting the bull in the fog. It reminded me of two-a-day football practices, up on the old football field back home in Chester.

We went out through the wire and down the finger. We went along the ridge to the northwest about two clicks. We then went toward the north, down the hill, and back toward Hill 861. It was real easy humping up on the ridge. The only bad thing was that we made great targets. After we left the ridge and headed back toward the hill, it was a lot harder to move. We moved slow and stopped several times. It was about 2000 and we were about 400 hundred meters from the hill. We stopped there until it was almost dark, then moved up beside the trail and set up an ambush.

It was darker than the inside of a cow. It started to rain sometime during the night and that made it even darker. Most of us had our ponchos with us, so we put them on and that helped some. I don't think we would have seen a gook if one had walked down the trail. We were all up under our ponchos and lost in our own thoughts.

We got the word to move back inside the wire just before sunrise. It's now 0644, and I'm hitting the rack.

December 18

I didn't get out of the rack until 1220. I wouldn't have gotten up then if someone hadn't gotten me up. A squad from 2nd Platoon was going out to do the same thing we did last night, and we had to man their bunkers on the line. It wasn't too bad, just sitting there in a fighting hole, looking out into the night.

I had seen in movies how the men in combat would say you never want to be the third on a match. We were lighting up cigarettes tonight, and you wouldn't believe how long it is from the time you light the first smoke until you light the third. I can see how a gook could get you lined up and shoot the third man. I'll never be third on a match—most guys won't.

I was thinking today about how I felt when we got back in off patrol yesterday morning. When I was out on other patrols or LPs I was more scared than anything else. The last trip out, I felt different. Maybe a little scared, but more fired up, angry, pissed off at someone, but I don't know who or why. It was a strange feeling. I wish I could talk to someone about it.

Not too much else to write about tonight. I'll just go to sleep.

December 19

I ended up sleeping in the trench last night. I had just gone to sleep when the LPs had some movement right out in front of our bunker. We jumped in the trench, just waiting for the gooks to hit us. We were on alert for a couple hours, but nothing happened. I was just about ready to head back to my bunker when the LPs said they had movement again. We stared hard into the night but didn't see a thing. Nothing happened, but I spent the rest of the night in the trench anyway. It wasn't any worse than sleeping out in the bush.

I moved back to my own bunker this afternoon. I spent most of the day working on the damn thing.

My squad has a patrol tomorrow. Who gives a shit? I'm tired and I think I'm ready for some action.

December 20

I was up at 0600 today. It was a good start to a better day than I had yesterday. Every time I opened my mouth yesterday I got my butt chewed. I tried to talk to the gunny about the bunkers, but he told me not to worry about it, in less-than-kind words. I was running my mouth about the patrol and pissed the Lt. off. I had better learn to keep my mouth shut, but that's history.

We went out at 0915. We moved down the hill toward the north. Then we moved along the wire on the east side of the hill. We then came back through the wire on the south perimeter of the hill. We got back in at 1540. We were looking for anything that might belong to a gook, or for gooks themselves. We didn't find a thing.

It's getting close to Christmas. We are going to have a Christmas cease-fire. I think it's funny that a country you are at war with and doesn't believe in God the same way you do will stop fighting while you celebrate a religious holiday. I'm not sure I trust the gooks well enough to get too far from my rifle.

I'm really tired tonight. I should sleep good tonight.

December 21

I just fooled around the area today. We didn't have anything to do.

Went down on the lines at 2100 and hung out with Corbett and some of the guys down there. We listened to the LPs for a while, but they weren't doing anything.

We are all getting real homesick. I don't know if it is because it's Christmas time or what. I know I would like to be back in the hills of West Virginia instead of these hills of Vietnam. One of the guys said he is thinking about shooting himself in the foot or someplace that won't kill him so he can get sent home. I want to go home too, but not bad enough to shoot myself. They were talking about a guy who was on Hill 950 and got shot in the ass. Everyone who was up there said it was an accident, but these guys think he paid the other guy to shoot him so he could get out of here. I told them that they could get court-marshaled for that. I don't know for sure, but a person might get the death penalty for shooting himself to get out of a combat zone.

Talking to those guys just made me feel worse. I'll go to sleep and be one day closer to going home.

December 22

I didn't sleep well at all last night. I had just gotten to sleep, and the sound of a grenade going off woke me. I jumped up and started looking around. I couldn't see a thing. About this time, another grenade goes off. By this time I'm about to shit my pants. Then I hear a lot of yelling. It seems one hole thought he saw something so he threw a grenade. The next hole sees the grenade go off, so he thinks we're getting attacked, so he throws one. Finally someone realized what was going on and got everyone under control. I didn't enjoy the fireworks a bit. When you stop and think about it though, it was kind of funny.

Didn't do much today. First squad ran a short patrol. They didn't see anything. They were back inside the wire by 1600.

Talked to Sharp (full name and service number not available) a while this afternoon; he is due to "go back to the world" real soon. I don't think he wants to go out on any more operations.

I hope I get more sleep tonight.

December 23

Slept pretty well last night.

We had a recon patrol fly up here from Khe Sanh today. They are going out from here tonight. I once thought I'd like to be in the recon; but, going out like they do, I don't think I would like it anymore. One guy said he heard that intelligence is expecting all the hills to get hit pretty soon. They think the gooks will hit the hills all at the same time. I hope I'm off this hill before it happens.

Other than the recon plane flying over, there wasn't much happening today. I'm going to try to get some sleep.

December 24

Here it is Christmas Eve. I was thinking back on all of the other Christmas Eves I have spent in my twenty years of life. I don't think I have ever had one that was as lonely. But most of the guys feel the same way I do, so we just kind of put it together and do our own thing. I had my Christmas tree down at Khe Sanh, but I couldn't bring it up here on 861. Maybe just as well—I might feel worse looking at it. I received a lot of letters from people I don't know. I guess our names are given out some way. It was nice to get all those Christmas cards. One girl said she was sharp-looking. Maybe I'll write back to her.

I took over second squad today. Some of the guys in the squad are Huskey from Rochester, New York; Taylor [Buddy(service number not available)] from Chicago; Green from Austin, Texas; Beal [Peter J., 3449129] from L.A.; and Parker from Philadelphia.

We watched recon get hit out in the valley today. It went on right below us. We saw this Huey working out, and it fired several rockets into the side of a hill. Then we picked the whole thing up on the radio. We listened to the recon saying that each one of them were down to their last magazine of ammunition. Things looked pretty bad for them. It was like watching a movie from way up on this hill, except we all knew Marines were getting killed and wounded. We saw the CH-46 go in, and it was catching all kinds of hell but it got them out. It gave us a real feeling of helplessness to sit up there on top of the hill and know that we couldn't do anything to help them. I mean, the distance was too great to try and get down and help them.

My squad was sent out on an ambush tonight. I was more than a little worried about it. This was the first time I was in charge. We went about 400 yards outside the wire. We went out at 1900 and came back at 2300. It was after dark when we went out, and it was so dark you could hardly see where you were going. Parker had some idea of where we were to go, so he was leading us out. It wasn't easy but we got out there and got set in. Then we just sat there and waited and waited and waited. At 2015 a grenade went off behind us, between us and the lines. We thought, "Man, what the heck is going on! How did a gook get past us?" This scared the living hell out of us. It really scared me to think we were pinned down outside of the wire and couldn't get back in. Our first thought was that the NVA had moved in between us and the fence and getting back through the wire would be impossible. It was really a scary feeling for a while. When we came back in, we found out that it had been thrown from the lines. One of the M-60 gunners thought that he saw something moving, so he threw a grenade. Lucky for us it was far enough away that it didn't hurt anyone. I had a little talk with the man from guns about knowing where friendlies are located. He felt bad about it. He was just so scared he didn't know what else to do. He probably saw the moving trees. We were also told that maybe the NVA were probing the lines, but I don't think so. If they were probing the lines, we would have heard something from them. I just can't imagine them coming between us and the wire and not being heard or seen. They would have had to come up the trail that we were on, so we would have been able to ambush them. Hill 950 got hit again last night; they had eight grenades thrown in and two wounded. I don't know what it is like up there, and I sure hope that they don't send me up to find out. Sharp, Tim, Moe, Lanny, Smitty,(full names and service numbers for these Marines not available) and I drank a bottle of scotch; not exactly the best way to spend Christmas Eve, but at least the five of us got to sit around and tell stories. I thought about trying to get them to sing Christmas carols, but I don't know them very well and I didn't want to act like a geek. So Christmas Eve is over, it's not my best Christmas Eve, but maybe it won't be my worst either.

December 25

It's a beautiful day here. We had our Christmas day, and it was really something special. First thing this morning, Sharp, Moe, Smitty, and Lanny left. That was kind of sad, but they are on their way back to the world. They left on one of the choppers that brought up hot chow. The choppers that brought the chow had Santa Claus posters on the front of them. One had "Merry Christmas from the Ugly Angels" on its side. It was neat to see. It's not raining, the sun's shining, and you can just see forever. It's just beautiful. We've been outside all day, just kind of messing around, and we had a spotter plane fly over playing Christmas carols. Sitting there listening to that was kind of sad; kind of melancholy, I think. You know that back home, the family is opening the Christmas presents, and I hope they are thinking of me. But it is just not the same. This is not the first Christmas I have spent away from home. This is the first Christmas that I was in a position I couldn't at least get on the phone and call them. But I'm sure they are thinking of me. I hope that they are praying for me too. There is nothing like being home for Christmas. When they flew overhead playing that Christmas song, "I'll be Home for Christmas," it made us all feel pretty crummy. A couple of the guys said something about trying to shoot it down. I don't think anybody really would. It was nice to hear the Christmas songs anyway. If you have to spend a Christmas in Vietnam, I guess this was as good a place as any.

We got the word late this afternoon that we should be heading back down to Khe Sanh tomorrow. We are going to hump back down. I'm looking forward to it. I won't miss this hill very much. It does look better than when we came up, and a little safer too, but I'm glad to be leaving.

I feel really sad right now. I wish I could do something about it, but I know I can't. Hopefully it will be gone tomorrow when I won't be thinking of Christmas so much. The only thing I can do about it now is lie down on this cot and quietly cry myself to sleep.

December 26

It started out as a rather strange day. They got us up and told us to get our gear packed and be ready to move out. We were going back to Khe Sanh and then we were going to go out on a big operation. Normally we travel the Amtrak trail, which is a trail that has two tracks where the Amtraks have been digging it up. It's pretty easy walking. Instead, we went off to the north side of the hill. No one goes off the north side of 861 to get to Khe Sanh. We went down around the finger and off the edge and came back through the bush. I don't know what they were doing. I don't understand why they made us do that. At first we thought it was something of a joke and we were going to meet the Amtrak trail. But we stayed off the trail the whole way. Maybe intelligence had told them that there were some ambushes set up, and they were using us for bait. I do believe that there are some NVA in the area, and maybe that was what we were trying to do. We were just trying to find them. But we fooled around; went back and forth up over the side of the hills and down the valleys. Of course they told us if we see anything or spot anything to bring the lieutenant up and let him take a look at it. We didn't get back into Khe Sanh until 1730.

We are back in the tents on main side, but they told us tomorrow we are going to move out to the lines, Gray Alpha Sector. We will have the Gray Alpha Sector perimeter.

Something is up around here. I'd better get a good night's sleep. It may be the last one I get for a while.

December 27

Picked up three new guys today: Verschage [Raymond L., 2393922] from Rochester, New York; Geerdes [Donnie A., 2375606]—I don't know where he's from; and Markum [Robert B., 2360733] from Norfolk, Virginia. I really liked Bob right off; he is kind of a stocky-built guy. Looks like a good hard-nosed Marine. Ray's a little more quiet, and Don I don't know well at all yet. He's not going to be in my squad.

It's back on Gray Alpha for a while. The bunkers are pretty flimsy but we are talking about trying to get that taken care of. Maybe getting some better things built and putting some more wire out front. The way intelligence is talking, we had better get it done pretty quick. We do have the ARVN out in front of one section. With the ARVN out in front of the west section, we don't have to worry about that one. (Although some of the stories I've heard about the ARVN aren't good. If they get hit, they may try to get through our wire while trying to run away from the gooks.) The rest of Gray Alpha is open and we look right into the valley. We can see down toward Highway 9. If they wanted to attack, they would probably come right through there. We are going to secure that area pretty well with some trip flares and claymores. We might as well get this place built up a little bit; it looks like we are going to be here for a while.

December 28

We are back in the tents on the main side. It's typical Marine Corps. We didn't do much today. We were going to start working on the lines and the bunkers when word came down to back off the lines. We are going to go out on some operation. So they moved us back inside. I don't know who is taking over the lines, but I hope they do some work on them. When we left the perimeter there wasn't anybody there to take it over. I assume somebody is moving back down there.

It definitely fired us up when we got the word to pull back. We thought we were finally going to get some security and have a place to settle for a while. Then they drag us up here today and say nope, get your stuff and move back into the tents. You know, I worry about these tents a little bit. We were told to start putting some sandbags around them, and that is what we are doing—putting some bags around the outside, but it's no protection at all. These tents are just like living in a cardboard box. A mortar round would make a shambles out of one. Even a stray bullet could come through and hit you. The few rows of sandbags we are putting up around the outside might stop an AK round but nothing else. From what I understand, the gooks have some pretty powerful weapons now. I don't know if the sandbags are worth the effort. I don't feel real safe here at main side in these tents anymore. I'd much rather be out on the lines, providing my own protection.

December 29

They rolled us out of the rack bright and early, 0600. Everyone had to be ready to move out by 0800. They loaded us on CH-46s. Looks like it must be a battalion-sized operation. They flew us out to Old Mother or someplace near Old Mother. The first wave received sniper fire on their way in. When we came down we didn't get anything. Air strikes and flares set about 50 acres of grass on fire. It was really an ashy mess. At least the fire cleared it off so we could see in every direction, but it doesn't leave you much for protection. There wasn't a thing to hide behind. It just burned the hell out of this whole hillside.

The new men really got a workout. It's a shame they didn't get more time to get into better shape before they came out here and started doing all this humping. There was no time. We had to bring them out. Markum was on point, and I thought he was going to die. The heat was really hard on him. We were cutting through some pretty thick brush where he had to chop and cut to get through, and that was pretty tough on him. I switched off with the guys up front, each taking turns; that way, everybody was doing the same thing. My squad did pretty well; I was really pleased with the way things went. We humped for about four hours. We moved very slowly and stopped several times. There was no contact that I know of.

We set in on the north side of this hill. Right now it seems pretty quiet. I hope it stays that way. I had to send out one LP. Somebody else had an ambush. It's a nice night; I'll sleep good.

December 30

It was the second day in the field on this operation. Things were pretty quiet last night. No problems with the LPs, so I slept well. We pulled out at 0830 and had only moved about 300 meters when Bravo Company—who was on our right flank—got hit. I was right down in the middle of a swamp and didn't like it at all. I got down just the same. I could hear all the firing, but I couldn't see anything. Second and third platoons set up an ambush where we thought the gooks might come through, but didn't get anything.

We finally moved out again after an hour. You could tell that there are NVA in the area. The big brass seemed to know it too. We were moving very slowly and we were moving very carefully. We were not moving like we have in the past, when we just walked along the trail, skipping and smoking cigarettes and really enjoying ourselves. We were very much aware of what was going on around us. The point people were really watching what was going on in front of them.

Deschaine is crazy. He thought he saw something and fired a burst out into the trees; he didn't get anything, but hell from the skipper. The skipper was so upset about it, I thought he was going to make him police up his brass. I think Deschaine just wanted to fire his rifle.

After we set up the ambush and didn't get anything, we moved on across the river about 200 yards and set in. Just as the second platoon was moving into their positions, starting to relax and take their gear off, a gook jumped out of the bush and opened fire. He hit Goff [Carl, 3327146] pretty bad. I guess he may lose one of his legs. It hit him in the leg, in the right arm, and in left side. Smitty, the corpsman from my platoon, went up to help out. He said he wasn't sure who the other guy was but he thought it was Beringsume[Kenny, 2311383]. He was hit in the arm and may lose it.

I don't think I am going to get too much sleep sitting here tonight. I feel really strange. We are in a relatively good position. I feel pretty secure about it. We're sitting here against the side of this hill and we are fairly well protected on all sides. I know there are North Vietnamese in the area and they are moving. They are building up something. This is a search-and-destroy operation, and we are out here looking to see what we can find. I am reasonably certain that we are going to make contact with the NVA before it is over.

December 31

Didn't have any contact last night, but didn't sleep well either. I don't think anybody did. There was a lot of movement around us. Puff was working out off in the distance, down in the A Shau Valley further north of us. There must have been some gooks down there. We started moving out, heading back toward Khe Sanh, slow, just like we did yesterday, and being very cautious. We got some movement off to the front of us someplace. I heard some rifle fire, so they had us stop. We scattered out and set in. We must have been there for a couple of hours and didn't hear a thing. Nothing happened. Finally the word came down to move out. This time we really took off. We were heading straight back toward Khe Sanh and we were moving. We weren't nearly as cautious. We were safe, I guess, but we weren't taking our time. We were moving as fast as we could.

We got back in just in time for beer call. Here it is December 31, you have to have a beer or two on New Year's Eve. I thought of the three other New Year's Eves that I have spent in the Marine Corps; we have had some pretty wild parties. Tonight we got two beers. Two warm Ballentine beers. The paint was worn off the cans, they had been banged around so much, but they tasted real good just the same. We got together and told a few lies about how great we were back in high school and how great it's going to be when we get back to the world.

We are still staying here in the tents, which I don't like very much. So what, we'll make the best of it. It's New Year's Eve and we have a couple beers. What more could you ask for?

January 1

What a way to start a new year. I had just gone to sleep when Deschaine got me up. He wanted me to see the jack-offs the guys were setting off down on the lines. At first he thought they were looking for gooks in the wire. Then he realized they were just bringing in the New Year. It wasn't all that wonderful to me. I would rather have been sleeping.

We were up by the medevac area this morning when they brought in a couple recon Marines. One of them was dead, shot right through the running lights. It wasn't a very pretty sight. The other one died on the chopper coming in, I guess. Normally recon tries to stay away from any kind of contact. The word was they walked right into a battalion of gooks. They were North Vietnamese regular army so they are pretty good soldiers. The word we got was recon tried to disengage but the gooks stayed after them. Someone at medevac said there are some dead guys still out there.

I think we left 861 in time. The gooks were probing the wire early this morning. The Marines found some battle dressings and some blood trails. I would say we got out of there just in time. Intelligence has been saying the gooks were going to hit the hills—maybe they were right for a change.

Ran into a little problem with some boot lieutenant; I don't know where he was from or what he was doing here. Some of the guys in my squad were just fooling around the area. They weren't causing any trouble or doing anything wrong. He comes up and starts bitching at them; I don't know what he thought he was doing. I told him, "This is my squad; if you have a problem you come see me and I'll take care of it." He started to say something to me, then he remembered this isn't the States. He probably just came into country and thought he was a badass 2nd lieutenant. I feel sorry for his platoon. Lieutenant Simpson backed me up so I felt pretty good about that.

I'm going to sleep early; I'm really tired and I don't have any watch.

January 2

The day started about the same as any other. I got up and went to chow this morning, and things tasted pretty good. I was glad to get a hot meal. Everything around here looked pretty good.

One thing I don't like about this place—and being back here in the tents on main side—is that when it gets dark it is time to go to bed. We do have electric lights that are on some of the time, but they have been keeping those off. Intelligence seems to think there may be some North Vietnamese around the area, so we keep it dark at night.

My squad got the job of burning the shit today, and it is really a nasty job. We have wooden outside toilets; we don't have any flushing toilets or running water in this place, so every morning, you have to pull these cut-in-half 55-gallon drums out from under the toilets. Your pour kerosene on them, and you set them on fire. Then after they burn a while, you take a stick and stir it up to keep it burning. It is one nasty, disgusting job. It is funny because when the other squads would have to do it, you sit back and laugh at them. When you come back after burning them for a couple hours, you can still smell it. The stuff gets in your clothes and it really stinks. So it was not a good day; my boys were not really happy today, and neither was the squad leader.

Not a whole lot to write about tonight. It's getting dark, so it must be time to go to sleep.

P.S. I must have hit the rack around 2030 hours. At about 2100 I was awakened by what sounded like rifle fire. I got up and looked outside the tent. I could hear bullets whizzing over my head. I got the troops up and we went out to our fighting holes and just waited. We could hear all kinds of fire and see all kinds of flares. There were a couple of choppers out there where 3/26 has set in. They haven't been there long, so I didn't know if they have their wire up or not. I haven't been out there so don't know what their place looks like. There was definitely something going on out there. We got back in the tents about 2400 hours, so I am not sure just exactly what did happen. I am sure I will find out in the morning.

It's 0035. I think I'll try to get some more sleep.

January 3

Larry, I hope you had a happy birthday wherever you are. I am sure you are at home. I just wanted to let you know that your big brother is thinking about you. I hope Mom and Dad didn't make you eat peas. Bet Mom made you one of her delicious birthday cakes. That would sure taste good tonight.

I found out what all the shooting was about last night. It was 3/26 getting five NVA confirmed kills. It seems the LP that was out saw some movement. He got them to fire a 60 mm mortar illumination. They saw seven NVA around the wire. A reactionary force went out and got five of them. They didn't get the bodies back until this morning. I went over to the hospital to see them. I took some pictures. Those were the first dead gooks I've seen. When they went out this morning and got the bodies, they found their belts had been cut, so whatever they were carrying was taken off them. It may have been some kind of explosive to blow the wire. Maybe they were going to attack us, I don't know. When they cut their belts they took all of their weapons except one AK-47, two pistols, and a couple chicom grenades. The two gooks that got away stripped the bodies. They stripped everything so we wouldn't know what they were doing. But I wouldn't be surprised to find out that they had some banga-loer torpedoes, or maybe some things to blow the wire so they could come through. Maybe they were just going to set it in last night and blow it some other time. So 3/26 does have some wire up out there, though not real strong. It was a good place for them to attack because they could have come right on across the base from there.

A platoon went out and picked up the blood trail of one of the gooks that got away. They followed it for a while, but they couldn't stay on it well enough to see where he went.

It really makes me feel crummy: we take our whole battalion out, patrol for three days, don't get a thing. What's worse, we take two WIAs. 3/26 just sits in the lines and gets five confirmed. You know, I don't think this war is really fair to 2nd Squad, 1st Platoon, Delta Co. 1/26.

I believe I am changing. I am not as afraid as I was at first, and I'm looking forward to getting into it with the gooks. I don't spend as much time thinking about dying as I used to either.

It's getting dark, so it must be time to hit the rack.

January 4

Not too much happening today; just kind of sat around most of the day. Got paid; I only took $50 because I don't need very much money. It's not real money anyway; it's NPC. That gives me enough money to play poker.

I did take the squad back up to 861 and brought down the company's gear. We flew up in a CH-46. When we left 861 last week we humped off the hill, they didn't want us to carry all of our gear, so we went back up and got the rest of that stuff and brought it down.

The word is that we are going out on an operation tomorrow. We are going out with Alpha Company, but I don't know where we are going or anything else. But the CO told us to be ready to go tomorrow morning early.

I hope I get some sleep tonight. It may be a while before I'm back in this rack.

January 5

We just got set in for the night. It has not been a real happy day. We humped out here to 689; it took us nine hours. Again we are on patrol; we are moving real slow and very conscious, looking for things. I don't know what they expect; we move a little bit and we stop. Alpha Company is in charge so I don't know exactly what they think we are going to do out here.

I am not real happy where we are setting in for the night. We got out to 689 and set in near the bottom of the hill. I really don't like their perimeter. Our position is out on the edge of a finger, which is not bad. We are probably in better shape than everybody else here. I think we set in too far down the base of the hill. I don't like the way we did it. I don't like the way Alpha set us in here. We have one machine gun with us and we just set it aiming right down the trail that comes up the finger. I don't know how long we are going to be here, but I hope we get out of here real quick.

It was really a nasty hump out here, too. It is hot and really sticky. It just seemed like it took us forever to get out here. Usually it takes us about three hours to hump this far, but today it took us nine hours. Again we are really looking for things; I don't know what we are looking for. But someone must be looking for something.

This reminds me of the hump out to 420 with the XO that time in November. I didn't like where he set us in that night either. We made it OK that night; maybe we'll be OK tonight.

January 6

We made it through the night. I was really concerned, though. I still didn't sleep very well out on that finger. Of course, we were in better shape than most of the other guys. I can't believe the gooks didn't hit us. If they're out there any place, they must have thought it was some kind of trap or something. If they wanted to, they could have come right down the hill and just massacred the whole bunch of us.

My squad and I ran a little patrol that covered about 1,000 meters. We slowly humped along the base of 689 and on out toward Khe Sanh Ville and back around. We just made a big loop. We had to hump through some pretty big brush at times; we had to chop it out. I had Markum on the point, and he did a nice job. He really chopped the stuff down and we got through it OK. Once we circled around Khe Sanh Ville and started back, we were on the trail, so it wasn't too bad then.

We headed back into Khe Sanh about 1130 and we really humped it. My squad was on point and we just ran that Alpha Co. into the ground. They could hardly keep up with us. We stopped, just once, right outside the base. We were leaning back against these trees when—all of a sudden—we heard this crash behind us and here came these wild boar. Geerdes had one run right into him. It really ripped the back of his pack up but it didn't hurt him. It really knocked him for a loop. We all took a couple shots at them, but we didn't hit them. There were three of them. Wouldn't it be funny if Geerdes got a purple heart for being injured by a wild boar!

We got back into Khe Sanh at 1530 and just fumbled around the rest of the day. Had some chow and played some cards. Everyone is pretty tired. I think my squad and I are going to get along OK. I like all of them and they seem to respect me enough to do what I ask them to do. I hope I don't have to make any life-or-death decisions with them.

January 7

I didn't do too much today. I had two company formations. They just make us put our gear out there and stand around and look kind of silly.

We had this boxing smoker this afternoon, and it was really strange. I had to fight a guy named Mclaren [Roland L., 1950108] from guns. They stopped it after about two minutes. Lt. Chapman wanted me in there with this kid. I was hammering him. I was really hammering him bad, and they just let it go. I was really afraid that I was going to kill him, but I think the lieutenant wanted it that way. He wanted to see this kid get his butt pounded. I didn't know what he had done; maybe he made some people mad along the line.

That was about all we did today. After the smoker, had chow and just kind of hung out for the rest of the day. I got some things ready for this operation tomorrow, cleaned my rifle, and gathered up some extra ammo and chow. We got some mail today. I received four letters—two from home, one from Jeanne Lafferre, and one from some girl I don't know. It's really nice to get mail. Jeanne and I grew up together. She lived about 200 yards from me. We never dated like boy and girlfriends, but we were the best of friends. We always talked to each other about our boy and girlfriends and just about anything else we needed to talk about.

January 8

We pulled out of Khe Sanh about 0700. The second platoon had the point. First platoon was second, with the colonel and the CP group between my squad and Corbett's. It wasn't bad going out. Set up for the night west of Hill 689.

I have to admit I was a little bit shook up. It was a little nerve wracking. The way we were moving just bothers me. We were not humping like we were going from one place to the next. It is more like we were out there looking for something—trying to find things. We would go a little bit and stop; then we would go a little bit more and stop. We just really seem to be looking for something. Maybe there are gooks in the area and they are just trying to get us to flush them out. I don't know, but I am a little nervous setting in out here tonight.

They do have us set in where we can see the gooks if they would attack. My squad is on the perimeter next to Corbett's. Everyone seems a little jumpy. I won't get much sleep tonight.

January 9

We spent most of the day humping—just moving along like we have been. We moved over to Hill 557 and set up on the western finger. I am in a hole with Corbett's squad on my left, so I feel pretty safe about this place. It is not the greatest position to be in—-a lot of open area between squads. We cut down some trees to give us a little better field of fire.

I was really surprised we didn't have any contact today. I could just feel it. We were walking along knowing the gooks were out there some place. The worst part is that the jungle is so damn thick; they could be 20 yards from you and you couldn't even see them.

We set up for tonight on 557. We have our machine gun sitting so it's aiming down the trail. It's not too bad of a place. I think we will be OK set in here for tonight. We will see what happens tomorrow.

January 10

Today was Mom's birthday. I was thinking about her a lot. I'm going to send her a card. I had to make it. We don't have any place to buy one around here. I sent her a letter five days ago, and I hope she got it. Mom, I'm thinking of you on your birthday.

Well, well, well, we finally got to see a little bit about what war is like. At least the way it feels—we weren't lucky enough to have any contact. They sent us out on a platoon minus early this morning. My squad had point, and Corbett's was right behind me. I put Hall [William J., 8346010] on the point; he had a hard time. You know, he is physically able to do it; I can't understand why he had so much trouble. He had to chop through some pretty thick brush, so maybe that was it. I moved Markum up, and he did a good job. Of course he always does. He's the kind that gets in there and just chops and moves. He really takes pride in being on point. A lot of people don't like being on point. They are afraid it is a place to get shot. The old salts around here say, "The gooks will let the point go by, and then hit somebody on down on the line." We found a pretty well used trail. Lieutenant Simpson, Henry [Larry T., 8300510]—the platoon radio operator, Hall, and I walked up a ways to check it out. You know, it was really a strange feeling. We were just walking real slowly. Hall was on point and he was up there looking every which way. I was right behind him, the lieutenant was behind me, and Henry was behind him. We just walked real slowly; kind of moved up a little way and sat down. We are using hand signals, all the things they taught back in ITR. It was the first time I ever really got a chance to use anything like that. We didn't find anything, except and old NVA shoe. It was the only thing that was there. It looked like it had been there for a long time. We got back inside the perimeter about 1430.

They told us we would be staying here on 557 for a couple of days if we got resupplied tonight; we did, so here we stay. The choppers just came in and dumped the stuff out. It is pretty easy getting resupplied. If there were gooks in the area we were thinking maybe the choppers would draw there fire. That didn't happen. So we will just set in here for tonight. I feel pretty good about it.

January 11

We just hung around the area all day. Our squad really skated today. Corbett and Deschaine ran a company minus with third platoon. They didn't get in until 1745. They didn't have any contact, and they were just about as upset about it as we were yesterday. We are all getting itchy; we all want to have some contact. We have been trained to be fighting Marines, and we all want to find out what it is like to be in a firefight.

I had radio watch from 2100 to 2200. I had to wake up Delta Six. We got a call from the listening post, and Delta Six said to wake him up if we heard anything. So we woke him up and he listened to the LP. But it was no big deal, nothing came of it.

When I went out to check the lines, I walked up to my hole to see who was on watch; found Huskey. John and I talked a little bit. We shared some personal things. We are both a little nervous, a bit anxious about what is going on out here. On my way back to the hooch, I caught Parker asleep. He is a nutcase anyway; nothing seems to bother him. But he is responsible for all of our lives, and he isn't going to sleep on watch. I banged him around a little bit. I tried to put the fear of God in him. I thought a little fear might wake him up. The next hole was OK, but in the next hole, Stripling [Ronald F., 2345665] was asleep. Stripling is a good kid; he works hard. He really seems to do a good job. I know everyone is tired, but we all have to stay awake when we are on watch. At the next hole, the man was OK; he didn't have his boots on, but he was awake anyway. I know we all like to get our boots off when we can. The next hole was the gun hole; the gun was there, but nobody was there on watch. I found the man in the next hole. He was in the hole just shooting the breeze. I told him that that section of the line needs to be covered, so he moved back where he belonged.

It seemed that everybody was really lax today. Maybe we feel more confident than we should, or maybe I am just a little more nervous than I should be. I really feel that we are in a bad situation. We're in a place out here in the boondocks, where we could get attacked at any time. I want to make damn sure that the people are at least awake. They might not be able to stop everybody, but by God, at least we will be awake to give it a try. I don't know how well I am going to sleep tonight.

January 12

We were getting ready to head out for Khe Sanh when the gunny came around to check out the area. He gave me hell because our area was so messed up. I found Stripling's helmet; I don't know what he was doing or why he left it lying there. I found a flare and some other junk lying around. You know, it is hard to believe these guys just don't care about their equipment. I guess maybe being a football player, I learned that my helmet is my protection. I make sure I have mine around even if I am not wearing it all the time. At least I am carrying it with me. Everything we leave around is going to tell the gooks something about us. Besides, I don't want the gooks to have our flares. So I had to make sure everyone had picked up their junk. Gunny jumped on me and I jumped on them. Shit flows downhill.

The hump back in wasn't too bad. We made it in at about 1500. Got to clean up; this was the first time in a couple weeks that we had a chance to take a shower. I got a shower and a shave, and I feel pretty good. We had steak for supper! That meal went down well; it was real groovy. We got some beer about 1700. Again we got the good old warm Ballentine. But it was beer and we just sat around and shot the shit.

I'm going to sleep. I feel pretty good tonight; nice and clean for a change. I'll sleep like a baby.

January 13

What a surprise I got today. I took over right guide for our platoon. I didn't even know we had a right guide. There must have been somebody doing it; I don't know who he was. I never heard from him. What a right guide does is simple: he is in charge of bandages and bullets. Anything the platoon needs from supply, he gets it. So he is kind of a supply sergeant. It is not a bad job; I don't have to go out on patrol and stuff with the squads now. I will have to go out when the platoons go out, but it won't be too bad of a job. It really surprised me, though. I haven't been in country that long, and I would have thought there was somebody around here senior to me. But that is the way the Marine Corps does it. Whoever was promoted first gets the job first. So it is not going to be too bad.

I just hung around the area today. I didn't do much. We did a little work on the wire. Of course, we don't get any beer; it is all gone.

I'm going to hit the rack early. We'll see what happens tomorrow.

January 14

I drew some utilities for a couple of the troops. They said they needed some new ones. We went down to supply and got them. Not much going on.

The word came down we are going to be put on a sparrow hawk and be ready to move out at any time, so the troops are getting stuff ready to go. My job is to see that they have plenty of supplies, and it looked like everybody was supplied and ready to roll.

The word is we will stay here in these tents and be ready to move out at any time. They say we could be sent out to help recon or up on one of the hills if we're needed up there. I guess they fly us out and we do what we have to do. I can handle that.

I may have a little trouble sleeping tonight. This sparrow hawk is exciting.

January 15

I found out the first thing that is bad about this job. You don't have anything to do. They took us off sparrow hawk and took all the squads and put everybody out on working parties. My job is just to hang around the area. So that is what I am doing. That is what I did all day; I just kind of hung around. I did a little reading and just fooled around. I'm not sure I can handle this doing nothing. All my life I've been busy. I like to have work to do. The gunny told me I'm not to be out on any work details with the troops. He said I'll find something to do. There is not much happening here.

I played some cards about 2000 with Heath, Crawford [George C., 1983304], Tenner, and Warner (full names and service numbers not available for these two Marines). I didn't do too well; I lost $10. It was one of those games you just play and have some good times.

I hope I can find something to do tomorrow.

January 16

I just continued to hang around the area today. I couldn't find anything to do. They took the troops out on some work parties. I don't know where they went. There are different places around the base that need work.

They told us to start wearing our helmets and flak jackets. It is really hot and nobody wants to do it. But they told us to at least keep them close to us. They must be expecting something.

I didn't do too much; just kind of hung around. Played cards tonight until 0030; I won $30 tonight. Last night I lost $10 and tonight I won $30. So now I am up $20.

The funniest thing happened. I was lying down here in my bunk before we started playing cards. I was about half asleep. I knew somebody was messing with me. I thought they were tying my shoe laces together. All of a sudden I realize that my boots are on fire. I jumped up and started to stomp my foot on the floor. I realized they had packed C4 in the cleats of my shoe. Thank God one of the guys grabbed my leg and kept me from smashing my foot down on the floor. If he hadn't grabbed my leg, I would have ended up blowing my whole leg off. Of course, it was real funny at first. When everyone realized what could have happened, it wasn't so funny. I didn't think it was funny at all. A couple of the guys apologized. They said they didn't want to see me get hurt. I understood; in a combat area, what can you do for laughs? You don't play tiddly winks. I have heard of guys pulling the pin on a grenade and throwing it to each other, counting to five or so, then throwing it into a bush. A game I've played myself is shooting razor blades at each other. You take your shirts off and shoot double-edge razor blades at the other guy's chest. If you stick it in him or cut him, you get to keep shooting. If not, it's his turn to shoot at you. You really cut your thumbnail up.

God, I hope I find something to do tomorrow.

January 17

I had a rather busy day today. I was able to find some things to do. It was just paperwork, but at least I was busy. I filled out these forms on all the guys in the platoon, what their rank is, had they been wounded, and stuff like that.

I am real glad we left 861 when we did. They were attacked last night and took four WIAs. They had one on 881. So it looks like the gooks are really starting to move in tight. Intelligence tells us that we are supposed to get hit tonight or tomorrow night. But I don't know, they never seem to be right.

2/26 is moving out by 3/26. They are really expanding the base. There is not much protection out there. They are going to string some wire, I guess, in the hope that they can stop something. There's not much protection, just a field and some small trees. They are going to have to dig their own fighting holes and just hope for the best.

I put it to S/Sgt. Sykes today about my meritorious promotion. I think I deserve it. He said he thought I did too since I was doing the job of right guide. I should be at least an E-5 sergeant. So he is going to send it off for me. He said it is on its way. I'll just keep my fingers crossed.

I played cards again tonight. I won $25 tonight. So I am starting to get ahead. No one cares how much they win or lose. There isn't anyplace to spend your money anyway.

We had an AO plane crash at the end of the runway this afternoon. I don't know if it was hit or what happened. I was sitting on the edge of the bunker, and all of a sudden, you could see the smoke from where it hit. I didn't see it go down, but they say that both people on the plane were killed. I didn't even go up to see it. I feel sorry for their families, but there wasn't anything I could do for them.

I think I'd sleep better if we were out of these tents.

January 18

We are still here in the tents. About 1200 they saddled us up and told us to go down to Blue Alpha Sector, which is part of the trench line off to the west. We went down and just laid around all day, doing nothing. I don't know if they expected us to get hit during the day or what. I really don't think the gooks are going to attack this base during the day. I think if they are going to hit us, they are going to come at night. They told us we would be back in the tents tonight. So here we are. I don't know what is going to happen.

I started playing some cards again tonight. I got interrupted about ten times. It seems every time something happened, somebody needed me for something. It's kind of funny though, just the other day I was pissed because I couldn't find anything to do. I guess it's being busy when I want to be busy.

It's not been a real good day, although no one has been killed today, so I guess it is not all that bad. I feel something is going to happen. There is a lot of tension among the troops. I'll not sleep well tonight.

January 19

When I got up this morning, everything looked about normal. They told us to move down to Blue Alpha Sector again. We moved down there and just hung out, watching the lines and shooting the bull until about 1300. We then got the word to come back up to our area and saddle up. We were pulling out on a sparrow hawk. India Company 3/26 had gotten hit, and they needed some backup. So we got our stuff together, got ready to go, and nothing happened. Again it is hurry up and wait deal. We sat at the edge of the runway and waited for the word to board the chopper that was on the runway waiting for us. We just waited for the chopper to fire up and take us over there. Somebody just changed their mind. I don't know what happened. We are the last to know what happens. Anyway, we didn't have to go. So we are back in the tents again tonight.

I had the strangest feeling come over me while we were sitting on the runway. I guess it was a real case of fear. I have never been in a real firefight, but I knew if we went out I was going to be in one. I knew some of the guys would be killed, and that scared the shit out of me. I know it's going to happen one of these days, and part of me is looking forward to it, but part of me is scared as hell.

I played a new card game with the guys and won about $100. So it was a pretty productive day as far as cards go.

I still have this feeling something is going to happen. I hope I can get some sleep.

January 20

I didn't get much sleep last night. Whiskey Company began firing tank rounds at about 0230. We hit the holes. We came out of the holes at 0300. It wasn't long until the B-52s started dropping bombs. They couldn't have been more than a couple miles away. So it was back in the holes again. When the

B-52s drop their bombs, they shake the ground all around us. I've never been in an earthquake, but I'm sure it must be like this. We were in the holes until 0350, but I couldn't get back to sleep when we did go back into the tents.

While I was down in the hole, I checked it out. I don't know what it would stop. It might stop an AK-47, but I don't think it would stop anything else. We dug a new bunker today. We put sandbags around it and sandbagged the thing in pretty good. But I really don't think it is going to be worth much. If they started hitting us with any kind of artillery or mortars, this new bunker is not going to protect us much.

Today I got a taste of what the viciousness of war really is. We saddled up to go out on the sparrow hawk that we should have gone on yesterday. They told us to get ready to go. We are going to go out to India Company 3/26. They had taken 40 WIAs. I don't know how many KIAs they took; they never tell us that. They were hit hard during the night. We didn't go!

The word came down later why we didn't go. I found out from intelligence that they had a gook lieutenant turn himself in sometime during the day. He said the action on Hill 881 was diversionary, just to get the troops out of Khe Sanh, then they were going to come in and attack the base. I say bring your ass on in here and we'll see if you can take this base!

You could really sense that something was going on. All the people I talk to—the officers that I see roaming around—are really thinking about something all of the time. It is not the kind of laid-back, relaxed atmosphere we had here a month ago. So maybe the gooks will hit us. I don't know what is going to happen for sure.

I guess the worst thing I saw (or maybe the funniest thing I saw) today was that the AVRN had three gooks tied with a 50-foot rope, and they were hanging upside down off the bottom of this chopper. They were dragging them around through the trees. I saw one guy hit a tree—it ripped his arm off. It was sad but kind of funny. I'm not sure how I feel about it. I found out later that is how the AVRN handle the North Vietnamese regulars when they want to find out something from them. They just torture them. I think the Geneva Convention says we are not supposed to treat prisoners that way, but we just let the

AVRN do this to them. It's their war and their country, so I don't really care. The chopper started north toward the A Shau Valley and was dragging them toward the trees. When he came back there was only one gook left on the rope. I don't know if it tore the other ones off or what happened to them. I guess it was kind of sad in a way.

Word just came down that the North Vietnamese have already taken Hill 881 North. If they took 881 North, 881 South is not very far away. I will be sleeping with one eye open tonight.

I put the diary away and I tried to go to sleep. I couldn't get to sleep. It was really strange. Off in the distance, we could hear tanks. I could hear the tracks on the tanks. You talk about being scared; I don't want to meet any tanks. Deschaine and I were talking about it, and at first we thought they must be ours. We walked down to headquarters to see what was going on and to find out if they were our tanks. Of course, they said they couldn't hear any tanks, there weren't any tanks in the area. But we knew if we were real quiet, we heard tanks. There is no doubt in my mind. I am anxious to find where these babies are. It looks like I won't find out until tomorrow.

January 21

What a night. Hit the rack at 2200 hours and went right to sleep. At 2300 hours I was awakened and told to saddle up. We were going out to get a recon unit that was in trouble near Hill 689. Recon radioed in they were pinned down by a large North Vietnamese army force. They were trying to break it off, but no matter which way they moved, the gooks were there. The squad had a couple wounded and felt that if help didn't get there soon, they would get wiped out. Thank God we didn't go. It was darker than the inside of a cow. That is the worst thing about this place. When it is cloudy at night, there isn't any light at all. Even back on the farm in West Virginia there was some light at night, but here, there isn't any. We just sat in our gear and waited. We stood down and got back in the rack about 0030.

I was rolled out again at 0415 to go to Hill 861. The word was 861 was being overrun. I heard later that a battalion-sized attack force was in the wire. Hill 861 is not a big hilltop—you couldn't put a battalion inside the wire. Thank God again we didn't go.

I took my gear off and walked over to the head. It was a three-holer, but it was full, so I just leaned against the side while I waited and talked to Deschaine, who was on the inside. It was 0457. I was facing northwest when all of a sudden, the whole sky turned red. It's really funny now because I know the sun comes up in the east. But for a second, I thought the sun was coming up over there. I couldn't believe it! The whole sky west of Hill 881 was on fire. Before I could take one step toward my bunker, the first rocket hit. The concussion picked me up and I went flying through the air for about 10 feet. It seemed like I was in the air for the longest time. As I was flying, I could see the ground below me, but it looked very strange. I didn't think I was going to die, but I thought, It's going to hurt when I hit the ground. I hit the ground on my side; it didn't hurt too badly. I started screaming, "Incoming!" and slid into my hole. Everyone was jumping to the nearest hole. Some of the guys from my platoon weren't in our hole, and some of the guys from other platoons were. Most of us didn't have our rifles. Some guys didn't even have helmets or flak jackets. I started to crawl out to get my rifle, but the incoming was like rain. One round hit so close, it threw dirt all over me. We just sat there and prayed. This was the first time I had ever been under attack like this, and I didn't know what to do. I didn't know whether to go out and look for the other guys and maybe get blown away or stay put and get blown away when some gook threw a grenade into my hole. I knew this had to be the attack intelligence had been talking about. One guy from 2nd Platoon was so scared he started to cry, but no one said anything to him because we all felt like crying. So I just stayed in the hole and waited until it stopped.

They rocketed and mortared us until about 0700. God was really on our side. A round hit right beside our new bunker but didn't go off. When we blew it later in the morning, it blew the whole side out of the bunker.

I couldn't believe what the base looked like when I came out. The entire place was in shambles. The rockets had hit the ammunition bunker and blown our own rounds all over the place. All of the tents were blown apart. Everyone in them had to have been killed. I found out later that some guy who had just gotten into country yesterday had a rocket hit near him and cut his lower jaw off. I don't know if he made it or not. The CO's area got hit bad too. The gooks must have had it zeroed in. Everywhere, something was burning, and every two minutes, something would blow up. I thought to myself, "It's going to take one hell of a police call to get this place cleaned up." It really made me feel good when I saw the flag was still flying.

The gooks can't be too smart; they should have hit us with a ground attack. I don't know what it was like out in the lines, but here, everything was confused and messed up. Nobody knew where anyone else was or what to do. I don't know how many people were killed or how many were wounded, but I didn't see too many casualties.

About 1000 hours, we got the word to saddle up. We were going down to Khe Sanh Ville. We went out through the Bru village, and no one was around. I had only been in the village a couple of times, but there were always people around. It really seemed strange to see the ville empty. I don't know where the villagers were hiding. I never saw any holes.

We went out over Hill 471. I didn't know why we had to hump over the damn hill. It would have been a whole lot easier to go down Highway 9. Hill 471 isn't real high, but it is steep and hard to climb. We had been out there a couple of weeks ago, and the trails were rough.

We were in a column. My squad was the last squad to reach the staging area. We were near the open field by the bridge. It was then that Corbett brought this man up to me. He was dressed in a flannel shirt, blue jeans, and tennis shoes. He was white, but I don't think he was American. Corbett handed me a note the man had given him. It was addressed to a captain whose name I didn't recognize. The note said, "If you want to see the commander of CAC Company this man will take you to him." I took the man to Lieutenant Simpson, who was going to take him to Captain Spencer. I had a real strange feeling about this man. He never spoke. Where did he come from? How was he able to walk up on us so easily? I later asked Corbett about him, and he said that the guy just came up behind him from nowhere.

Just as we started to go out on the open field, we got the word to pull back. I found out later that a couple of gooks from CAC Company had gotten out at the ville and told Captain Spencer we were headed into an ambush set up with 50-caliber machines aimed across the open field.

I am not sure that my drill instructors, Sgt. W.L. Roach, Sgt. B.W. Floyd, or Sgt. R.L. Malone, (no full names and service numbers available) would have been too proud of the way we headed back. It was like every man for himself. Assholes and belly buttons were running up Hill 471 as fast as they could go. It was raining and the ground was slick and we could hardly keep moving up. I heard these funny sounds around us and finally figured out it was bullets hitting the mud. The gooks were shooting at us from somewhere. I didn't see anyone get hit, but we were all scared as hell.

When we got to the top of 471 and started down the other side, I saw four Hueys working out on the north side of Highway 9 at the bend where you head up toward the base. I found out later that the gooks had set up another ambush out there. If we had gone out or come back on Highway 9, the whole company would have gotten wasted. Did you ever wonder why things go the way they go? I was pissed because we went over to 471 and not down the highway. If we had used the highway, I would probably still be lying out there.

We got back into Khe Sanh at 1715. We have two gooks of the CAC Company with us. We got them some chow, and a couple of guys tried to talk to them; I stayed away. For all I knew, they were North Vietnamese regulars. I didn't like having them around, and I was glad when some guy from headquarters came and got them.

Corbett and I cleaned out the bunkers good enough to sleep in tonight. We are still getting a lot of incoming, so we sandbagged the hole in the side well enough to keep shrapnel out. I don't think we will be here long anyway, so no sense doing too good a job. It has been one hell of a day. I am too tired to be scared, so even in a bunker with part of a side missing, I should sleep pretty well tonight.

January 22

I had a good night's sleep last night. Even though the side was gone out of the bunker, it wasn't too bad. We slept pretty well. We are going to build a new bunker today, Henkel [Gene, 2007687], Corbett, and I. We don't know where we are going to do it exactly. We are going to try and do what we can with the one we have first. We may end up moving down on the lines, so we don't know for sure yet what we are going to do.

We had a few mortars and small-arms fire try to get the planes along the runway today. You could hear them hitting out there on the runway. I don't know how much longer we are going to be able to use this airstrip. 1/9 got part of their troops up today. They are out there trying to lay some wire and trying to get some kind of security, get some holes dug. Somebody said they are going to bring up some big equipment to try and help set it up out there.

So far we have had 13 KIAs and 40 WIAs here. 861 had 100 NVA dead in the wire this morning. When they got up this morning, they were all just stretched out all over the place. It looks like what they tried to do was just come charging in. The first few just fell over the wire; the next ones ran across the top of them. We were lucky we didn't lose the hill. If the gooks had gotten inside the wire, we could have very easily lost it.

From what we have been told, intelligence must have passed the word down to our CO and he passed it down to us. It seems that the NVA want to take Hill 861. They want to do that first. Then they are going to bring a regiment down from the north and one regiment from the south up the opening at the end of the airstrip, which is probably the least secure area on the base. They want to keep one regiment reserved. They want to take Khe Sanh, Camp Carroll, Dong Ha, and all the way down to the coast, then bargain for peace. At least that is the word we are getting. But I'll tell you right now: they are going to have a hell of a time taking this base. We are not going to give it up easily. With 3/26 and 1/9 out here and 1/26 here inside the base, let them try. We have a few South Vietnamese soldiers—I don't know how strong they are going to be, but they are controlling one part of the lines. I do know that there are some real crack Korean Marines out there that won't take anything from anybody. The gooks are going to find it awful tough to take this base—I don't know about Camp Carroll and Dong Ha. I am telling you right now: Khe Sanh combat base isn't going to fall to the Goddamn gooks.

We'll be sleeping in our three-sided bunker one more night.

January 23

We didn't have many incoming last night. I didn't get up this morning until 0800, so I really slept pretty well. We had a few incoming rounds today. It seems like they are trying to get the planes on the runway. Every time a plane comes in or just tries to land, they start bracketing the base to get the mortars out there on the runway. They also fired in some 175 mm rockets like they fired in the other night. They make some big holes in the ground. We didn't get any incoming near us at all today, so that made us feel pretty good. The base is a real mess, though. The company office is gone. The post office is gone. The PX is gone. I mean, they just leveled the place. When you look out across the base and try to remember things that were there before, it is really hard to tell. Everything is just blown up or burnt up. They did a job on the base. But I will tell you what: they didn't hurt very many people. We were lucky. There were people killed and wounded, but it wasn't nearly what could have happened. Everybody on this base is very jumpy. You stick your head out the bunker, look around, and do what you have to do. But you stay low and you travel quick. Our movement is getting called the "Khe Sanh quickstep," which you use or just don't go outside at all.

Another day is over and I'm one day closer to being back in the world.

January 24

I slept pretty well last night. I don't think we had too many incoming.

Doug, Gene, and I redid our door and dug a little more out of the inside of our bunker. We had to change the door; we realize that if a gook just ran past and threw a hand grenade in, there was no way to stop it. It would roll straight down in. So we put a turn in the door in a place with probably two-foot-thick dirt, where if a gook would throw a grenade down in there, it would explode and hopefully wouldn't hurt us on the inside, depending on how big it was.

We had a few incoming and saw a few air strikes. The gooks must be coming up pretty close to base. We had some F-4 Phantoms and F-8 Crusaders doing some bombing right out near the edge of the base. Those little A-1E Sky Warriors do a nice job too. They get in real close. I'd be real happy to have them around if I got in the shit out in the field.

At about 1700 hours the gooks just started to unload on us. They must have hit us with 25 rockets and 75 or 80 mortars. The company had two WIAs. That is not too bad, though. That was over in 2nd Platoon. 1st Platoon and 3rd Platoon didn't get anybody hurt. As far as the guns and mortars, we didn't hear anything from anybody over there. So I guess they are all OK. God was on our side again tonight. They let up for about 20 minutes. It just seems like they will let up and everybody will say, "Well, it's over with for today." We will start moving around a little bit, and then they hit us again with about 50 rounds of mixed artillery and rockets and mortars. It just keeps you on edge all the time.

This would be a good night for a ground attack. It is dark, and if they have been waiting for a chance to do it, I think this might be the night. So we are really going to be on watch. When we sent out the listening posts earlier, I was real aware and made sure those guys were the ones that could do it. So, hopefully, if a ground attack comes tonight, we will be prepared for it.

The bunker is a little safer tonight, but I won't take my boots off to sleep.

January 25

Well, we made it through last night. It wasn't too bad. We had a few incoming that woke me up, but we just stayed down in the bunker and felt pretty secure.

We got the word today that intelligence says there are three divisions of NVA out there instead of three battalions. This is the regular North Vietnamese Army—well trained—and good fighters. There are a heck of a lot more troops in three divisions than there are in three battalions.

We spent the day working on our bunker between mortars and rockets and so forth. We would just get our heads out and start doing something and Bang! we heard them coming. Hill 881 could hear them firing, so they passed the word over the hotline. It's really kind of funny; we have a speaker set up over on main side, and all of a sudden you will hear, "Incoming! Incoming!" and everybody hits the deck. By the time you get hidden good, it will hit the ground. So it is kind of nice. I wish that 881 could pinpoint them, though. Then we could drop something on them and knock the mortar fire off anyway.

Hinkel, gave me a real scare today; I thought he was cracking up. He was just pissed off. He didn't really say what it was, but finally, I figured it out. He was just angry and fed up with this incoming.

Webb's (full name and service number not available) not doing too well. He is one of these guys that can't stand the constant pressure of these rockets and artillery. You just can't do anything; as soon as you start moving around, they start firing. The incoming is getting to him real bad, as it is all of us, but I think it's starting to hurt him more. Intelligence did say that they are supposed to harass us and just keep dumping this stuff on us until the 27th. I guess on the 27th they are supposed to lay it on us real thick and hit us with a ground attack. Where they get this information, I don't know. I suppose that it's from some of the gooks that have surrendered. So far, I can't say a whole lot for intelligence. They kept telling us that we are going to get hit, and we never have yet. I hope they are wrong this time too.

The bunker is looking good enough to take my boots off tonight. Corbett thinks I'm nuts for doing it, but I sleep better with them off.

January 26

It was really pretty quiet last night. We did have a few mortars, but, you know, I'm getting used to it. They didn't wake me up at all. We worked on the bunker again today. We are really starting to make this place look like home. We dug some more dirt out and reshaped the door a little bit, but there were enough mortars to keep us near our holes. Sykes got a piece of shrapnel in the chin; Dennis [Mitchell O., 2207332] in the arm—neither hurt bad.

We started something a little new tonight. I think we are all scared. Somebody once told me there are no atheists in a foxhole, and I really believe that. So Corbett, Stripling, a couple of other guys, and myself did some praying in our bunker tonight. I am the only Catholic, so I said I was going to say the Rosary. I did that tonight. I think one of the guys is Jewish, so he is going to have some prayers to say. Doug and a couple of the other guys who are Protestant are going to have some prayers to say, maybe even read the Bible or whatever. You know, I haven't been real religious over the years that I have been in the Marine Corps. But I think tonight it was really something to have us all here and to say the prayers and just ask God to protect us. So I really hope he hears our prayers, as I think he will, and keep all of us safe.

Everything seems pretty quiet tonight.

January 27

It wasn't too bad of a night. We had a few mortars come in close. I woke up once, but it really wasn't too bad. The day turned out to be pretty shitty. 2nd Platoon really caught hell. They had five WIAs and one KIA. Urizzel (full name and service number not available) had both arms and a leg blown off; it was really sad. We helped carry him up to Charlie Med. As we were carrying him up there, I realized a piece of his head was even gone. He died at Charlie Med just after we got him up there. I didn't know the guy at all but I knew who he was and had seen him around the area. It was tough to see anybody that messed up. It was the first time I have really gotten close enough to see somebody who has been hit. It was just about like it was in the movies. Just about what I expected. There was a lot of blood. One of the guys picked up his arms and carried them up there. I don't think there was anything they could do for him. He was dead when we got him there. He had lost an awful lot of blood, and I am sure the shock was unbelievable. No one knew how he got it for sure; a mortar or rocket must have landed right on top of him.

We had a few incoming, but less than other days. Maybe the gooks are running out of mortars. I don't know, but I can hope.

We are supposed to be ready to get hit tonight. They say that it is really going to get rough again tonight. So with what intelligence knows, it probably won't happen.

We said the Rosary at 1730 tonight. All the guys came over, and we said it in our bunker again. It's really a time we can relax a little bit. It makes us all feel better. I think after we have had some prayers, we all go back to our bunkers feeling safer. It's only been five days since this incoming started, and everyone is feeling the pressure. So a few minutes of prayer helps.

I really feel bummed out tonight. I feel a lot of hate for the gooks coming up in me. After seeing those guys wounded and killed today, it really pisses me off. The incoming is getting to me too. I would like to see us go out after the bastards. Anything would be better that just sitting here day after day.

January 28

We didn't have many incoming last night. But artillery worked out most of the night—firing, it seemed like, every three or four minutes. I slept worse than any other night since I have been here. I would just get to sleep and artillery would fire or something would happen, and I would wake up again.

Luckily, we only had a few incoming today. There was even less than yesterday. We just bided our time around the area today; we did a little work and tried to police up the area here a little bit.

2nd Platoon got two gooks—one dead and one alive. But the one that was alive lost his leg, and I guess he was just running his mouth like a river. He wanted to tell them everything they wanted to know. I suppose like most of the situations they weren't going to do anything for the leg until he had talked a little bit. I can't imagine losing a leg. He was probably losing a lot of blood, and he wasn't a bit afraid to talk.

Intelligence told us again that we should get a heavy mortar and rocket attack tonight. Intelligence reminds me of the story about the kid who cried wolf. We are all sleeping down in the bunker pretty low, just the same.

We said the Rosary in my hole again tonight.

I haven't felt good since yesterday; I keep feeling like I'm going to throw up.

January 29

I slept a little better last night. Even though artillery fired most of the night, it seemed like it didn't bother me as much. It is pretty quiet around here today. We only had a couple incoming. It seems like they just fired enough today to let us know that they are still out there.

I took 20 men down to the west side of the base to work on the wire, and it wasn't a pretty sight. It was awful down there. They flew over one time with a helicopter spraying something. I don't know what he was spraying, but it was some kind of liquid. I suppose it was some kind of spray to keep the weeds and stuff from growing. They got some on us, but when we came back, we washed it off. No one seemed to be any worse the wear for it.

We definitely have no Tet truce up here. You know, I am really glad. When we have a truce or cease fire, all that the gooks do is reinforce themselves. They regroup and get ready to attack us again. So I am really glad we don't have a truce up here. I know throughout the country they're having it, but I guarantee that here at Khe Sanh we're not.

I had the Rosary in my bunker again tonight. Felt a little better today.

January 30

It wasn't too bad around here last night—fairly quiet. But about 0500 this morning Puff was really working out down around Khe Sanh Ville. He was down there for a couple of hours. I don't know what happened or what he was trying to shoot at, but he was definitely clearing out the area.

We went down to work on the wire again today. We stretched some more concertina wire and put in a few land mines—a few anti-personnel mines. We set a couple claymores. It wasn't too bad of a day.

We had only about 10 rounds of incoming again today. We had one guy killed and two wounded on the base today.

Some of the guys, including myself, are getting a little anxious to get off this base and go looking for some gooks. I don't think Marines are designed to work in a defensive position.

I'm really tired tonight—I hope I can sleep.

January 31

Not too much happened on the base today. We only had a couple of incoming rounds. We worked on the wire down on the west side again. We strung more wire, and we are really getting that built up. I don't know if they think the gooks are coming in on that sector or what. I don't know exactly what they are trying to do down there. They have 20 yards of nothing but dirt—plenty of open area to see the gooks if they tried to attack.

We tried to get out to the water pump while we were down there, but we couldn't get out. As soon as we started out, we were hit with incoming. Lt. Simpson decided it wasn't worth the trouble. We haven't been able to use the pump for a couple of weeks, so I guess we'll have to continue to have water flown in.

It really makes me nervous when we are down here. We are right against the base of the hill line that Hill 950 is on. It seems like the gooks could be in the woods someplace and just take potshots at us and pick us off one at a time. So far we have been real lucky and haven't had anyone wounded while we're working.

We got beer tonight for the first time in a while. We got 15 cans per platoon. I brought back 15 cans; there was a bit of a tussle for it. A couple guys didn't want any, so we divided up the 15 cans, and everybody got a little bit of it. There wasn't much to go around, but everyone seemed to enjoy it.

Every thing seems pretty cool. I should sleep OK.

February 1

Great day! They got us up early this morning at the usual time, about 0800. I had my breakfast; we are just eating C-rations now, so you can eat whenever you want.

We went down and worked on the wire again. They brought us a new type of concertina wire that doesn't have the barbs on it like barbed wire. This had razor blades on it, and it is really sharp. They issued us some leather gloves, but they really don't do much good. You have to be really careful; several guys got cut up trying to put this stuff out.

This afternoon we came back up, and I strung some electricity wire from over where the old tent used to be down into our bunker. It's pretty nice to have electricity for a change. We have one bulb just kind of hanging there. But at least we have electricity. So at night if you want to read or just sit up and talk, you don't have to burn candles. It's kind of neat.

Some young Army lieutenant came by today. I don't know who he was; I never saw him before. When he came by, we were all sitting there by our bunker. He had a cake that somebody had sent him, and he said he didn't want it and wanted to know if we wanted it. So we took it and split it up among the guys. That was kind of a neat treat for us today. I found out later he was with the ARVN.

Only problem with electric light, it's hard to go to sleep with it on. We have guys on watch at different times, so we leave the light on all the time. Like everything else, I'll get use to it.

February 2

We just hung around the area today. Not too much to do. We did hold a police call around the area. We just sat around shooting the shit most of the day.

One thing did happen, though: they brought us in some water so we could take a shower. This was the first shower I have had since all this mess started on the 21st. That was kind of nice. You know, you don't really appreciate being able to take a shower every day until you can't get one. I am sure that we all stink pretty badly. But you know you get used to it. You don't even think about it. I am around these guys every day, and some of them have gone without a shower longer than I have. I didn't notice it—didn't notice them smelling. But I did notice the white faces after they washed them. The red clay dirt here just cakes into your skin, face, and everywhere. After you take a shower, you look almost pale. I think it is a part of the climate here. The red clay just soaks into your skin and you end up looking like a red man.

We had about five incoming today. But they got lucky today; they hit the right spot. There were nine killed—four of them from the Army. It really pisses me off; the bastards killed the Army lieutenant that was over here yesterday. The guys over there said a rocket hit right on top of his bunker. We went over to see it. It looked like he had about 10 layers of sandbags on top of pallets. It went right down through it. So it must have been a rocket round that came through. You know, I really feel bad. Here is this lieutenant over here yesterday, gave us cake and talked to us a little while. Seemed like a really nice guy. Today he is dead. That is one of the reasons they tell you don't make friends in combat. You just make acquaintances. I guess this is one of my acquaintances that died.

We got the word today from Lieutenant Simpson. He told us that they think the NVA will hit us tonight. It is dark and you really can't see anything. There is no moon and there are clouds. It is really dark, so it would be a good chance for them to hit us. They have got to remember we can see them just as well as they can see us.

I'll sleep lightly tonight.

February 3

We had several incoming last night. They woke me up. We worked on the wire again today. They are really beefing up that section down there. So I don't know, I guess they figure it is one of the places that the gooks will try to come in. We had several incoming mortars when we were down there working. I don't know if we are just in the right spot or what, but none of them seemed to hit real close to us. Nobody got hurt anyway.

I did get a little scare early in the afternoon. I was walking back from the company area, and a rocket hit right behind me (about 25 feet away). I never heard it coming. I got hit in the hand with a piece of dirt. At first, I thought it was shrapnel but it just hit my hand. In the same instant you feel it hit, you look. It was just a piece of dirt; it must have been something like that, because it didn't even cut me. I sure jerked my hand up to look. I have got to say God was on my side today. If I had been five feet further down the trail, I would have taken it right in the head and it would have scattered my head and brains all over the place. So I was real lucky. I don't want to come that close to any more rockets. The sound was just unbelievable. You don't hear it coming until after it hits. It hit and exploded, and I could feel the concussion from it just push me through the air, just like it did the morning of the 21st. It just pushed me or blew me along, and then I felt the pieces of dirt and stuff fly. Thank God it wasn't shrapnel, or I would have been dead.

Maybe the praying I have been doing helps. I'll keep it up. I hope I can sleep tonight.

February 4

We didn't have much to do today. We just sat around the area. You know, no one feels like playing cards or doing anything. We just sit around the area and talk and speculate on what is going to happen or where we are going to be tomorrow. The whole attitude of the troops has changed. We are here; we are supportive of each other, but we've gotten that attitude. It is like I was saying the other day about when the lieutenant got killed. We just want to be acquaintances now. We don't want to know a whole lot about each other.

That shows. It shows in our attitude toward each other. I know that everybody here would support me and help me, and I would do the same for everybody else here too. But I just don't want to get involved with anybody. It hurts when you see somebody get killed. There are people on this base getting killed every day.

We got about 25 rounds today. Thank God they all missed.

Mac, our forward observer, has a great job. He doesn't do much; he just sits over on the bunker with his binoculars and watches the area. He said he saw about ten gooks on the hill just this side of Khe Sanh Ville. He called in an artillery strike. He said it was one of the best artillery strikes he has ever had. He said they got the gooks the first shot. Of course, they bracketed the area a little bit and fired a few more just on the chance of getting a couple extra. They killed at least ten of those bastards today. That's ten that won't get a chance to kill one of us.

Not a bad day. I'll get some sleep tonight.

February 5

It is really boring here. We didn't do a thing all day today. We just put in our time. You know: you clean your rifle, you sit around, and you try to find things to do. We are back here in the support area. There is just not a whole lot to do. I wish I was out on the lines; at least then I would have something to do. At least they could send us out on patrol someplace. They ought to do something with us; it is really getting boring staying around here. I noticed the troops are getting more and more edgy. I think everybody's looking for a fight.

We had a few rockets and mortars today, about the same as yesterday. Not really a whole lot, but enough to keep us awake. Hill 700 got penetrated. That's where the 9th Marines are. They said they didn't take the hill, but they got inside the wire and killed 9 Marines and wounded 25. They sent some people up from 3/26 to secure the area. So I don't know exactly what it is like up there now. They said they had 108 NVA killed. The FOB area got rocketed and mortared about 2000 hours. They had some guys killed down there, but I haven't heard yet what happened.

This place isn't fun anymore. I just need a good night's sleep.

February 6

I got to play forward observer today. It is kind of fun seeing what we could do. See how good I could be at calling in the fire, plus seeing how they were at firing on my coordinates. We were working on the wire again today. We had a couple of mortars; some of them were getting pretty close. It just so happened, I was looking in the right spot and saw smoke from the tube. I got the lieutenant over there and we started looking at it and figuring out where it was. With a 50-caliber machine gun firing, you could see the smoke. It was really stupid. I mean, here in broad daylight they are firing at us. So lieutenant Simpson called in artillery on the tube, and I called in 81 mm mortars on the 50-caliber machine gun. You have got to help bracket it. The first time they fired on the 50 they were a little bit on the other side, so I told them to come back a couple of degrees and they came back and got good coverage on the tube. But they weren't real hot on that 50. They kept firing at it and missing. But it did shut them down. They weren't shooting at us any more. I don't know if they ran and left the area or just stopped so we couldn't see them any more. After we realized we weren't doing a very good job on it with the mortars, we had an airstrike called on the tube. A Cannabera came in and really did the job. The first drop was white phosphorus; it landed right on the tube. It couldn't have been better.

We had quite a few rockets and mortars along with some artillery today. Corporal Meade [Thomas A., 2283723] got blown away. I didn't know him real well, but it was one of those things. He was one of those military acquaintances that you meet. They said that he took it right up through the side of the face, and the bullet came out through the back of his head or a piece of shrapnel did. They think it was shrapnel from an artillery round. So there's one ex-Marine. One Marine less fighting here for us in Khe Sanh. Meade was a good kid, from what I heard. I talked to Heath about it a little bit, and he said that he really liked the guy. He hadn't been in the country a long time, but he was the kind of Marine that was going to go a long way. I wish I could have known him.

This place is beginning to suck! God, just let me get some sleep.

February 7

It seems like the powers that be know what it takes. So they let us hang around the area like we did today. Maybe in a couple days, they will move us off and get something else going. We just hung around today.

Things were pretty quiet until about 1600. Then the gooks started firing in several rockets and mortars. We are down in the hole just hiding out. At 2115 we got a red alert. A red alert means we are under imminent attack. So we thought, "Finally, intelligence has got it right, although they didn't tell us that we were going to get hit tonight." We thought that we had finally had it. Though we didn't see anything, we went out and hit the holes and stayed there for a while. We didn't really hear anything or see anything. Finally we got the word that there were three UFOs flying over. They picked them up on radar; they didn't know what they were. They were really concerned that maybe they were Migs or something coming out of the north, but they weren't really sure. They're still not sure, so they were probably our planes. But it gave us a real scare. It was the first time now that we have been called up on a red alert and got sent into the holes and really expected something to happen.

Something funny did happen today. I was over at the piss tube when up walks this person all dressed in combat gear, and asked to take my picture. It was a girl! Why she wanted a picture of me taking a piss, I'll never know. I told her to get the hell away from me. I don't know why those reporters are here anyway.

Maybe I'll get some more sleep tonight.

February 8

It was quite a night out where 1/9 is. They've been out there now for about a month. They took 24 killed last night. They have 3 missing and a good many wounded. They didn't know how many. It seems the NVA spent most of the night getting up to the wire. They must have started right after dark. They said there were better than a company of them. They got up to the wire just before daylight. They must have some kind of a preset sign; at 0400 they blew the wire and came screaming in. The Marines held only a part of the trench and one bunker, and the gooks ended up taking most of the rest of it. After they got some support, they drove them back out. I am sure the guys on watch were aware of it, but I wonder what happened to the listening post. They should have listening posts out in front of that area. Maybe they were killed, I don't know, but I'll guarantee you if one of my listening posts doesn't answer up on the radio, I am going out there to find out what is going on. I'll put some flares up or something. I can't believe they snuck all the way up to the wire, got that close, and were able to blow it.

Lang Vei Special Forces Camp got overrun by nine tanks. A few weeks ago, I knew that there were some tanks in the area; I heard them. I guess we called in air support and they got five of them. That is one of my biggest fears: being out here as an infantry Marine and running into tanks. I am just petrified of tanks. I don't know what I would do if I saw one of them. If we knocked out five of the nine, that means there are still four of them roaming around. Hopefully, we can find them. They brought a bunch of gooks up from Lang Vei too. I know some of them had to be NVA. There is no way that I was going to get close enough to find out. The army caught them with maps on their arms.

We had two artillery forward observers blown away. One was killed immediately; the other had an arm and both legs blown off. He was all but dead but was still alive the last I heard.

It is really bad when you get those kind of people killed. You don't know what has happened to them. You don't know what is going on. All you know is that the Goddamn NVA are coming inside the base disguised as ARVN. That's what keeps me from liking the ARVN a whole lot.

I really hate this place! God, please let me sleep.

February 9

We worked on the wire again today. Had a couple incoming mortars hit pretty close. I think we have been down there so much, they have us locked in. I couldn't see where they came from, so I didn't call in any fire on them. About an hour later I really wished I had. They put about five rounds in our lap. McCline (full name and service number not available) had his right foot blown off. We couldn't find any part of it. He lost it from about four inches above the ankle. He was lying face down with his feet spread out. If he had had them together, he would have lost them both. I was about ten feet from him with my head turned toward him. I saw his leg jump up and go to pieces. Parts of it flew all over the place. Trevino [Richard, 2341602] was lying beside him, and he got a lot of shrapnel in his body. He didn't look too bad. He should be OK in a couple of months.

I blame myself for those guys getting hurt. I should have called in fire on the tubes even if I couldn't see them. I didn't want to put up with the shit I would have had to take from the guns. I would have given them a rough estimate of where I thought the gooks were, and they don't like that. They like to know exactly where they are firing and if they get any confirmed kills. If I had called, I might have saved two good men.

What happened today is what I don't like about being in charge. I won't sleep well tonight.

February 10

We had a few incoming today, but not too many. Several hit in otters. They killed three guys, one blown completely up. We heard his leg, from the knee down, was lodged under a truck. The Corpsman couldn't get it out. He had to find some way to move the truck. I think there were six wounded.

I found out today I'm going on R&R. I put in for it a couple weeks ago and it came through. I'm going to Hong Kong. It wasn't my first choice; I wanted to go to Australia, but the gunny said they try to send the married guys over there. I'm sure I'll have fun in Hong Kong. Just getting out of here for a while will be great. I leave on the 12th, the day after tomorrow, if I can get out. That would really piss me off if I couldn't get out of here.

To hell with this war; I'm excited about R&R, and I can't sleep.

February 11

We had a pretty quiet night. We worked on the wire for a while today and didn't have any incoming while we were down there. Since I'm going on R&R tomorrow, I got to take a shower over at Charlie Med. I think that's the only place on the base with a shower now. That was the first one in quite a while, and it sure felt good.

Several of the guys put in orders for things they want me to bring back. Some guys want cigarettes, but most of them want booze. I'll bring back what I can.

I'm just hanging around, waiting for tomorrow. I sure hope I can get out of here.

February 12

Up at 0630 and headed for the airstrip. I wanted to get on the first thing flying, and I didn't care where it was going. A C-123 came in at 0925. She hit the runway, turned around, dumped off some stuff, and was ready to take off. Seven Marines, including me, jumped through the open tailgate, and she was on her way. She came in, landed, and took off under mortar fire. We laid face down on the deck until she was well up in the air. Once she left the ground she climbed almost straight up. I hadn't thought about it, but we could have been shot down. Wouldn't that be a bitch. There were some happy troops on board when the pilot told us we could get up.

I had to get to 1/26 rear in Phu Bai, and that plane was going to Da Nang, but I didn't care, I was out of Khe Sanh. Flew to Da Nang and caught a flight back to Phu Bai right away. I'm staying at 1/26 rear for the night. I got to take another shower, a hot one this time. Had a couple of beers, and they really tasted good.

I feel like I'm back in the real world. I bet I sleep really well tonight.

February 13

I was up at 0630, had some hot chow. Then I went over to dispersing at 0730. I took out $478. I could have taken more, but everyone I talked to about R&R said to take only around $500. I took $478 because that left my account at an even $1000. I caught a flight back to Da Nang at 1230. It's much easier to get to Da Nang than to Phu Bai. Went to the R&R center, and checked in for Hong Kong. I had some time, so I went to the PX, had six hamburgers, and drank three cokes. This place is just like the States. I needed a haircut, so I went to the barbershop while I was at the PX. The barber was a gook, and when he wanted to shave me, I wasn't too sure. I figured if he cut me I would just kill the bastard. I found out I wouldn't be getting out until tomorrow when I got back to the R&R center. I didn't care, because the days don't start counting until I get to Hong Kong. I get five days in Hong Kong starting the day I get there.

They had a place for me to sleep, so I put my gear in there and went to the Seabee club for a few beers. I'm looking forward to getting to Hong Kong tomorrow.

February 14

I was up at 0430. It really feels good to get cleaned up and put on some different clothes. Had chow and went back to the PX for some film. I bought a camera from this guy in guns who was heading back to the world. I want to take a lot of pictures while I'm in Hong Kong; I don't think I'll ever be back. I headed back to the R&R center, ready to leave.

I left Da Nang for Hong Kong at 1400. The plane was just like the one I flew to Vietnam on. We got to Hong Kong at 1630. We were indoctrinated at the R&R center. They told us all the do's and don't's. We are not to be in uniform at any time. That surprised me; I had been in several countries in Europe and you could always wear your uniform. They even put the whores in order of safeness. The ones in the bars are the cleanest, then the ones in the hotels. He told us to stay away from the ones on the street. They will give you something you don't want. The ones in the bars are the most expensive and the street girls are the cheapest. He said most guys start out with the bar girls while they have lots of money but end up with the street girls when they are almost broke. I don't know why he told me all that stuff. I'm a good boy!!!

I got to the Park Hotel at 1730. Checked in and bought a bottle of Cuttysark scotch. Drank most of it with a guy named Longbine (Russell, 2355351) whom I met at the R&R center and who was staying right down the hall. We drank to our being out of Vietnam for five days. The bellboy brought our bags up and took our civvies to press them. I didn't know how much to tip him or how much this money was worth. I just put out my hand with some money in it, and he helped himself.

I called home and talked to Mom and Dad. It was really nice to hear their voices. Mom said everything was fine at the farm. Bood had been home for a few days and she enjoyed seeing him. I told them I would call again Sunday.

I was ready to go out and hit a few bars. The first one was right across the street from the hotel. When you walk in, Mama-San comes up and asks if you want a girl. She brings them all over in front of you and you pick the one you want. I met a sweet girl named Donna Woo; I'm in love.

I got back to the hotel at 0300. What a night!

February 15

I didn't get up until 0900. I was feeling a little rough after last night. Russ and I went out to get fitted for suits. The Chinese have some really good deals on suits. I bought a mohair three-piece suit and another one just off the rack. We have to be fitted again later in the week. I will send them home so I don't have to take them back to Vietnam. I won't have much need for a three-piece suit in Nam.

We are just going to fool around Kowloon tonight. Went out to a few bars, checked out the girls. These Chinese girls are good-looking. Most of them can speak enough English to get by at least enough to do what the guys on R&R want.

I got back to the hotel at 0230. I'm a little high. I should have no trouble sleeping.

February 16

I was up at 0800. I took a tour of Hong Kong Island. The people at the R&R center make all kinds of tours and things available to us. We rode a ferry all around the island. It is a beautiful place. I liked the ferry ride the most. Maybe I should have been a sailor. There are some really big buildings on the island, and a big harbor.

I went back at the hotel at 1400 and went to sleep for two hours to get ready for tonight. I fooled around until 1900, then went out to a really decent nightclub. I was back to the hotel at 0200.

February 17

I slept really well last night. I was up at 0700 to take a tour of Kowloon and the New Territories. We went up to the Red Chinese border. We saw a lot of refugees and where they live. They live anywhere they can put a cardboard box. They call them resettlement houses. Many of them were living up on the side of this hill. The guide said they didn't care where they live as long as they are out of China.

I met an American girl, Carol Chambers, and her father, Ed. Carol seems like a nice girl. Ed keeps hinting about getting off by himself. I think he wants me to take Carol off his hands for a while.

Went back to the hotel at 1430 to clean up and rest for a while.

I left the hotel at 1800 for a night tour of Kowloon. We went to a really nice restaurant for dinner. The only thing on the menu I knew was fried rice and pepper steak. It was pretty good. We then went to a Chinese opera. I could have missed it with no problem. All the other people on the tour kept saying how wonderful it was, and I didn't want them to think I was some dumb hick farm boy from West Virginia. I told them I enjoyed it too. The tour then went to a big-time revolving restaurant-bar on top of some hotel. I had one drink and was ready to leave. After that the tour split up. Some people went somewhere, and some others, me included, headed for the Gaslight Club. I told Ed I would take Carol home if he wanted to go somewhere else. He thanked me several times and took off like a shot. We stayed and watched the show. We danced and had a really great time. We talked a lot about the future and what we would be doing twenty years from now. I really enjoyed Carol's company. It will make going back to Vietnam a little more bearable.

I was a perfect gentleman, took her home and was back in my hotel at 0430.

February 18

Didn't get up in time to make the tour we were supposed to go on today. I hadn't paid for it yet, so it didn't really matter. I just kind of fooled around Kowloon. I went to a flick. It wasn't much of a movie, but I'm just about out of money, so I couldn't do too much.

I went back to the hotel. I did have some NPC left, so I thought I'd try to exchange that with somebody. They told us when we got here to exchange all of our NPC and not to try to exchange it out in town. I walked up to a guy and asked him if he would change it. He was a corporal that works at the R&R center. He hauled my butt in front of the captain. I told him that they never told me anything about the money when I went through the R&R center. I lied a little bit, but they changed the money for me, so I had a few dollars left.

I went out to a couple clubs tonight. I just sat around bullshitting with a few guys. Not too much to do. I didn't have much money to spend, so I wasn't going to do anything exciting. I got back to the hotel about 2400, and I'm getting ready to go back to Nam tomorrow. I'm ready to go. I have two bottles of sake to take back. It's been fun, but I'm looking forward to getting back with the guys.

I want to sleep soundly tonight; I'll be sleeping back in the war tomorrow night.

February 19

I was up at 0600. Today my brothers Dan and Don had their birthday. I'll bet Mom had ice cream and a big cake for them. I wish I had been there to celebrate with you guys.

I checked out of the hotel and they loaded us all in cars and buses and took us back to the airport. We flew out of there and headed back to Nam.

I was back in Da Nang at 1145. I really wasn't in a big rush to get back to Khe Sanh because I wanted to see Darrel Pennington first, so I called 1st Marine Division Headquarters and found out where he was. His hooch was over by the rock pile. I went over there, spent some time with him this afternoon, and stayed the night. We drank a few beers and talked about old times. It was really nice to see Darrel, hear about his family, and hear how things were going with him. I had been first stationed with Darrel on the USS Hunley AS-31 in Scotland. We both came back to the States and were on the commissioning crew of the *USS Canopus* AS-34. Darrel taught me all I know about being a Marine. He was from South Carolina and took me home with him a few times. I got to know his wife and they were my family away from home. I'm probably alive because of the things Darrel taught me.

Tomorrow I'll get up and see if I can catch a ride back up to Phu Bai and back to Khe Sanh.

February 20

I'm up at 0630. Darrel took me down to the Marine Air Terminal. We said our good-byes. Although it was good to see him and spend some time with him, he had things to do and I was ready to roll. Signed up for Phu Bai, and I don't know if I had a chance to get out of here today or not. Went around and checked with the Air Force and anyplace that looked like they had choppers in the hopes of finding a ride. I stopped at the 235th VMF All-Weather Fighter Squadron to see some of

Bood's old friends. They were really nice. He must have been well liked while he was here. They talked highly of him.

I couldn't find a ride, so I went to the Mag 11 club. They had a real good show. They had some South Vietnamese girls dancing and singing. They were good, even if they did mess up some of the songs.

I'm going to sleep at the flight terminal tonight, and I hope I can get out tomorrow. I want to get back to the guys at Khe Sanh.

February 21

I didn't get up until 0930. I went right away to the terminal flight area and manifested for Phu Bai. I just hung around waiting. There just wasn't much going up to Phu Bai, and there isn't anything going from here to Khe Sanh.

I didn't make it today. Nothing was going, so I am sleeping in the terminal area to be ready first thing in the morning.

I went to the club just to kill some time. I drank a few beers and a bottle of brandy with a couple of guys from here on the base. They decided we'd head down to Da Nang City. Da Nang City is off limits, especially at night. The four of us talked this six-by driver, who was going over to the other side of the base, to give us a ride. We told him to slow down when we got into Da Nang City and we'd jump off the truck. When he slowed down, we jumped off. We no more than hit the ground when there was a mama-san right there waiting for us. She knew what we were looking for. She took us into this little hooch, and I met this real sweet little thing and it was quite a night. It was really cool because in the distance Puff was working out. I thought man, here we are in Da Nang City, and some gook could come in here and blow me away before I realized it.

We were really concerned about getting back out. If we got picked up by an officer coming through, we'd really be in trouble. We just snuck up to the edge of the road and waited. The road was built up on a bank, and it was just sand, so we laid on the edge until we saw a six-by coming. We waived him down; he stopped; we climbed on, and we rolled back through the gates of the base. It really wasn't too much trouble. It was a worthwhile experience.

I'm sleeping in the air terminal again. I really want to get back to Khe Sanh tomorrow.

February 22

I was up at 0800 and boy, did I feel bad. I can't believe what I did last night. The worst thing that could have happened to me would have been getting killed. Right next to that would have been getting caught down in that ville. I'm sure the CO would have been real proud of me. I guess it must have been the bottle of brandy that made me do it.

Went to the flight control and manifested for Phu Bai again. They told me they thought I had a shot at getting out, so I hung around waiting for a C-123. It took off at 1300. I got into Phu Bai and went straight into the terminal, looking for a flight to Khe Sanh. They told me there wasn't anything. Khe Sanh was taking a lot of shit, and I'd be lucky to catch a ride on anything, but my best chance was a chopper. So I went to every chopper line that was there, to see if anyone was heading in that direction. Every one said the same thing, chances weren't real good. They told me to keep trying, so maybe something would be going. So I hung around the air terminal all day.

I didn't make it, but hopefully tomorrow I'll make it. I'm staying at 1/26 rear for the night.

February 23

I woke up at 0630. Got some breakfast, went over to the air terminal, and manifested for Khe Sanh. They said they did have a chopper going out at 1500. I hung around the terminal, waiting. I read a magazine about the war. What a bunch of bullshit that was. It showed some guys from Khe Sanh doing the Khe Sanh quickstep. I hadn't seen any reporters up there for a while, but maybe they've been there since I was gone. We flew over Khe Sanh, but we couldn't land. Khe Sanh was under heavy mortar and rocket attack. It really looked nasty. There was smoke and dust and a lot of things on fire. We ended up flying all the way back to Da Nang, which really pissed me off. Now I'm back at Da Nang and I've got to go back to Phu Bai before I can get back to Khe Sanh. I went over to the Mag 11 club, had a few beers, but I really didn't enjoy myself. I just want to get back to Khe Sanh. My guys up there need me, and I want to be back with them.

I'm going to sleep at transit tonight and hope that I can get something out first thing in the morning.

It's been 11 days since I left Khe Sanh. I couldn't wait to get out of there. Now all I want to do is get back. When we flew over the base today I wanted to land so badly. I know the guys are taking shit, and I want to be there with them. I hope and pray I make it back tomorrow.

February 24

I got up 0630. I slept at transit, so I didn't have far to go to get signed up for Phu Bai. Someone said that the Air Force was going to bring in a C-123 to fly us into Khe Sanh. There's about 25 of us here waiting to get back there. At 1300 the C-123 came in, and all of us loaded on. The pilot told us we could just relax until he told us to get down. Then we would have to lay down on the floor. I checked the exits out. He said that if we were hit, he would try to put it down someplace in one piece if he could. I know the area around Khe Sanh, so that wasn't going to happen. If we get hit around Khe Sanh and this plane goes down, we are dead. There is barely enough flat ground around the base to land a helicopter, let alone something as big as a C-123. It was really scary. I wouldn't want to be in the air all the time. I wouldn't want to be a pilot or even a gunner on a chopper. I like to be on the ground. He told us what he had to do to be prepared to be shot down. To quote him, "We're taking this son of a bitch in." We were ready to go. We landed at Khe Sanh at 1530, and they were getting rockets and mortars. It was just like when we left. When we hit the ground, the plane spun around. The back door was already open, and a few guys jumped off right then. I waited until she slowed down a little bit and I got the word to jump off. I hit the ground running for cover. The pilot was shooting the juice to her, and away he went. He didn't think about stopping. He got her back in the air in less than two minutes.

I grabbed my gear and got the hell off the runway. I headed back over to the bunker, and the guys were really glad to see me. Hinkel and his squad have an ambush, so we're going to wait until tomorrow night to have a little party.

Things have been going pretty rough here. They said they took 1405 rounds yesterday. That's the most incoming they've ever had. 1405 rounds would just about cover every square foot of this base. They said things are so rough that no planes have been coming in at all. I was real lucky to make it back. I would like someday to meet the pilot who flew us in here today. I can't wait to see what happens tomorrow.

I'm tired, but I'm really glad to be back. Too bad Hinkle is not going to be here tonight, but we'll just have to wait until tomorrow to drink these bottles of sake and party with the troops.

I know I won't sleep well, but it sure is great to be back with my family.

February 25

Up at 0600 and just eating C-rations. We don't have any hot chow. I just kind of hung out with the guys all day.

Bravo Company went out on a patrol, so we moved over to cover part of their line, and it was the worst thing I've seen since I've been here. There were two platoons on patrol. One platoon walked into an ambush, and I guess it was just bad shit. The gooks had a horseshoe-shaped ambush set up, and it just wiped out the whole platoon. The second platoon was going to go over and try to reinforce them, help them out, and they ended up in the ambush too. A third platoon went out to get them, but they were pinned down. They couldn't get to them. We were just sitting on the trench line, watching the whole damn thing take place out there. A lot of the men were trying to get back into the base, just straggling in. They didn't come back to the gate; they just came straight to the wire and tried to come through where they could. It was really terrible to watch them come back in. We were down in Gray Alpha Sector and could see them straggling back across the field. We had bombed the area pretty good, so there weren't a lot of trees. Some of them didn't even have rifles with them. It was a nasty situation. They said there were 28 MIAs. One guy came back through the wire right in front of us, and a couple of guys went out to try to help him. He had been wounded, shot in the leg, but he was still able to move. I guess there were two other guys wounded pretty badly that made their way back in. This was worse than watching recon get hit the other day. We all were wishing we could do something to help them, but we couldn't. If the third platoon got pinned, we couldn't make it out there either. We just watched them come back in and went out to the edge of the wire to help anyone who came in that way. After the guys that were able to get out of there, someone called in air strikes on the area. I hope there were no Marines alive when the strikes started. If there were, they are dead now.

They moved us down to Gray Alpha Sector permanently, and it's not a bad area. It looks like it will be a pretty good area to fight from, although we've got some things to do to it.

Corbett, Fox, [Joseph L., 2349418], Hall, Huskey, Hinkel, Shortround, and I drank the sake I brought back. We were drinking it out of canteen cups. That's not the classy way to drink it, but it went down smooth. Just stood my first NCO line watch. I stood watch for 2 hours and 45 minutes in the trench. There's not much to do, just walk around and talk to the guys and see how things are going. Everyone was alert and ready to go.

The shit's really been happening around here, and we could get hit any time. Of course intelligence is the same as it's always been. They tell us all kinds of stories, but nobody really knows what's going on for sure.

I'm going to sleep in the trench. I don't feel good about sleeping in this bunker quite yet, but it's going to be alright by the time we're done with it. Thank God I'm home with my guys.

February 26

We had a pretty quiet night. Not much happened. The LPs did have some movement out in front of them, but I guess whoever was on NCO watch got the starlight scope and tried to look out there but couldn't find anything.

Today was Dad's birthday. I'm not sure what day of the week it is, but I hope he is home to celebrate it. I know Mom will have cake and ice cream for him, whether he wants it or not. Dad and I were never real close. He was always pretty tough on me. He made me work harder than anyone I knew. I always knew he loved me, though he never told me in so many words. Dad, I hope you were home and had a happy birthday. I love you.

They brought this big light down—they call it a nod—and the thing must be six feet in diameter. What we're going to do with it is set it up to shine out across the area in front of our lines. We can adjust it because it's on the back of a trailer. We will look through the starlight scopes, and if we see any gooks within rifle range or even within mortar range, we're going to turn this big light on and shine it on them, then just blast the hell out of them. It will be like shooting ducks in a barrel. I think it's going to be a good time, if we get the chance to use it.

I drew some more ammo and issued it out to the troops in our sector. The guys were really concerned about having enough. Many guys wanted more magazines. We got some guys carrying ten or fifteen magazines with 18 rounds in each magazine. They're weighted down, but everyone wants as much ammunition as they can carry. I have been working hard at getting people set up and getting all the gear squared away for them. Everybody wants decent utilities and plenty of ammunition.

The days since I've been back off R&R have really been flying by, and I hope it continues to go like this. The faster the days go, the sooner I get back to the world.

I just came off NCO watch, and I was out there for an hour and forty minutes, and it wasn't too bad. The only thing that did happen scared the hell out of me. It was really dark; you couldn't see a thing right in front of your face. When I would come up to someone, I would turn my flashlight on and see who it was. I was down toward Corbett's area and bumped into someone. I turned on my light and just about had a heart attack. I thought I was looking at a gook. I grabbed him by the throat and took him to the ground. Corbett started yelling at me and pulled me off the guy. It was a new guy named Wantanabe [Steve T., 2382806]. He is Hawaiian and looked a lot like a gook to me. After I got settled down, we all had a good laugh about it. I'm glad I didn't hurt the kid. I'm going to sleep in the trench again tonight, but tomorrow we should have the bunker ready to go.

February 27

We had another pretty quiet night. Not much happened. The LPs said they did have some movement tonight, but we weren't able to see them through the starlight scope. I was on watch, and I keyed the handset to question them, and they said the movement was off to the left front. I looked through the starlight scope, and I couldn't see them. I couldn't see anything. We thought about just turning the big light on and seeing what we could see out there, but we figured the company commander would get pissed, so we didn't do that.

I had the troops work on their bunkers and the trench line today. It's really building up strong. We put up more sandbags on the trench and dug it down deeper. You can walk through the trench now without your head sticking out. It's got to be seven feet deep in some places, so it makes it pretty nice.

I'll sleep in the trench again tonight. We still didn't get our bunker good enough to sleep in, but hopefully in a few days we'll be alright.

February 28

Up at 0745 this morning—I ate C-rations, so I didn't have to worry about going to breakfast. I had the troops work on the wire out in front of their positions today. We restrung some more concertina. Of course we have the ARVN out in front of us, and off to the left a little bit. I don't know exactly what's right out in front of us, except some small trees and underbrush, and some tents way out there. I suppose the gooks could come through there if they wanted to. We strung some concertina and put up a little more tanglefoot. I wouldn't mind putting up a few more claymores out there too. I'll see if I can get some from supply.

I had to bring in one LP tonight. I don't know if they were sleeping, but I couldn't get them to answer me. I had set them in, so I crawled out there, and that's the scariest part of all. You know they're sitting against a bush or a tree or someplace, and you have to walk up on them. I was down fairly low, because I didn't want the gooks to see me either. It was dark, but there is still a chance you can silhouette yourself and get shot. I walked out close enough to throw a rock at them, but they didn't respond. I thought maybe they were dead. Finally, I just hollered at them and told them to bring their asses in. I brought them back in, and I had a little talk with them. When I was ready to take them back out, Hemphill [Garry L., 2336028] begged me not to send him back out. He said he was just scared to death. I didn't get too pissed off at him. I took it easy on the kid. We're all scared, and I told him that. But he's got a responsibility, and I told him we trusted him. I told him that he's out there because he's the kind of guy we can depend on. I told him we're all scared but we've got to get used to that, and we've got to be able to do our job. He finally agreed and went back out. He's a good kid. I hope he makes it. You've got to use the idea of falling off a horse. If you fall off a horse, you've got to get right back on him again and get ready to go. So that's what I tried to explain to him. Sure he's scared, but if he goes out this time, maybe the next time when he's in a critical situation or someone's life is really on the line, he'll be able to deal with it a lot better.

I'm going to sleep here in the trench tonight and kind of keep one eye open. It hasn't been too bad, but you can never tell about this place.

February 29

Not too much happened last night. It was pretty quiet. I slept really well. They said the LPs had some movement but were still unable to spot anything. We didn't have to go on 100%, so no one woke me up.

We did have a little excitement, though. There's a little turn down here in Gray Alpha Sector, and the machine gunner on one side thought he saw something, so he threw a hand grenade out over the wire. Well, the guys on the other side of the little valley thought it was gooks coming in, so they threw hand grenades out there. Well, then someone else saw the hand grenades, so he threw one. I guess they threw six or eight hand grenades back and forth at each other before somebody realized what the hell was going on. It was just like what happened on Hill 861. Those kinds of things happen. When you're scared, you don't take any chances. I don't blame them. If I thought I saw a gook out there, I'd throw the damn things too.

I just fooled around here today and didn't do too much. I worked on the bunker and had the troops work on the trench a little bit.

We did have a C-123 come in that brought some new troops and some chow, I suppose. The plane had some engine trouble. When he spun around, he couldn't get it cranked up to get it in the air again, so they pulled it off to the side so the gooks would have something to shoot at. I guess the gooks fired at it most of the day. I didn't go over to see, but hopefully they'll get the engine fixed and get the damn thing out of here tomorrow.

I'll sleep in the trench again tonight.

March 1

I stayed up really late, shooting the bull with the guys. I didn't hit the rack until 0100. I slept for about an hour, then we were up on 100% until about 0500. The word is the ARVN had about seventy gooks out in front of their lines. I guess they were trying to get through. I think it's kind of funny that they haven't penetrated in front of either 3/26 or 2/26 or anyplace around the 1/26 lines. They did get though the ARVN lines a couple of times. I don't know if it's true or not, but if the ARVN got seventy, that's not too bad.

The troops are really looking for a fight. I remember a couple of months ago thinking that Marines aren't defensive people. We've got to be out looking for somebody. So I believe that the troops around here are really looking for a fight. If the gooks do cross the line in front of us, they better look out, because we're going to kick us some ass.

I didn't do much today, just worked on the bunker. I think things are going to be alright. Grothkof [Bill J., 2366224], Clatterbuck [Clay, 2365947], and Labsure (full name and service not available) got wounded today. Grothkof came back with just shrapnel in his chin, but Lab and Buck got medevaced. The guys that saw it said a 60 mm mortar landed right in the bed of the truck they were in, and it blew them right out of the truck. It cut them up pretty bad, but Groth said he thought everyone would make it. Hopefully they will.

I'm going to be sleeping in the bunker tonight, and hopefully I'll get more sleep than I did last night.

March 2

I really didn't get much sleep. I was up at 0025 on 100%. I stood my watch at 0345, then went down to my hooch and slept until 1100. It was great, nobody bothered me. When I did get up, I worked on the bunker some.

I met this guy named Breedlove (First name not available) (2231061) from West Virginia. When he came over he had two Chinese mercenaries with him. They were some bad-looking dudes. I don't think I would want to mess with them at all. They didn't say much, but of course they might not have been able to speak English. I was talking to him about buying a pistol. I'd like to have a regulation 45, but I can' find one around here that anyone wants to sell. He had a Smith and Wesson 38 and he said he'd sell it to me for 60 bucks. Breedlove is with the FOB unit. So I went to his hooch to get the pistol. FOB has some really outstanding bunkers. They look like they have spent some time on them. Of course, they're probably not like us, here one day and gone tomorrow. It looks like they've been there a while.

I'm going to sleep in the bunker tonight, and hopefully I'll get more sleep than I have been getting.

March 3

Didn't get a whole lot of sleep last night, but not too bad. We went on 100% about 2100 and were there for about a half an hour. It seems somebody threw a grenade like the other night, and they pulled everyone out of the bunkers. I went back in and hit the rack until 0430 and then had watch until 0600. I hit the rack and was sleeping good until Heath and Dr. Swagier came over. We visited a little bit. Of course Heath is an E-5 sergeant now, and he doesn't have to do too much. Doc Swagier is a really good guy. We just shot the bull, sat around, and watched the troops.

I got to shoot my .38 and my M-16 today. I fired them out over the lines. The .38 looks like it's going to work alright. It doesn't shoot real straight, though. Maybe I couldn't hold it straight, but if I use it more I'll be OK.

I had first watch and now I'm going to go to sleep in the bunker.

March 4

It wasn't too bad of a night. Gallager [Charles, 2395411] was on LP, and he went to sleep. When he came in, I chewed his ass pretty good. I think he'll be alright. He volunteered to go back out again tonight, and I think he's trying to show us that he really feels bad about going to sleep. I really like that kid; I hope nothing happens on the LP tonight. He's a good Marine; I hope he makes it out of here alive.

I had quite a surprise today. I had no idea that Sykes was going to leave. The company commander called me in and told me I was now the platoon sergeant. Deschaine's going to be the right guide. I'm pretty excited about it. I think I can get more work out of the troops than Sykes ever did. I'm really excited about being platoon sergeant, but there's going to be a lot more pressure and responsibility for me. Every time something happens, the top is going to be on my ass to see that things get straightened out. Of course he doesn't say much to the officers, so we'll just have to wait and see what happens. I'm afraid this platoon sgt. job is going to change me.

We're getting ready to build a new bunker, if we can get the Seabees to come down here and dig a hole for us. It's going to be right off the lines, and a hell of a lot better that the one we have now. But for tonight, the old one will do.

March 5

It was a quiet night. The LPs stayed awake and everything was cool.

I had to stay on the squad leaders to get their police call done today. They didn't want to mess around with it, because nobody wants to clean things up, but we have to. Like the gunny said, "If we turn this place into a shit hole, we'll act like we're shitheaded people." So we've got to keep the place cleaned up.

I just spent the day going around, visiting the troops. There doesn't seem to be a lot for a platoon sergeant to do, but I hope it will be like it was when I was the right guide—the longer I do it, the better it'll be. I know I can get more work out of these guys than Sykes ever did, and I showed that today.

A B-52 bombed just off the south end of the runway. The air was just filled with smoke and dust for an hour. It's unbelievable how much the ground shakes when those things drop, and there's a huge explosion. It's nothing like the nuclear bomb dropped in WWII, but it's really big explosions and a lot of smoke and dust.

It stayed clear up until about 2200 today. If we needed air support we could have had it. It was clear enough for the pilots to see us.

I really hope this monsoon will be over soon. I'm really getting sick of the mud and rain. Everyone would like to see the sun. Of course, when the sun comes out, it's going to be hot.

I think I'm going to like being platoon sergeant. There isn't a whole lot for me to do, but I think I'll learn how to deal with that. I'll learn how to drink coffee with the gunny and just sit around and bullshit with the staff NCOs.

We got the hole dug for our new bunker. A Seabee came down with a backhoe end loader machine and dug a nice-sized hole. I was afraid we would start getting a lot of incoming and he wouldn't get it done, but the gooks held off and he got finished. I hope we can get it livable in a couple of days. For tonight, I sleep in the old one.

March 6

It was a quiet night last night. There didn't seem to be too much happening. The LPs and everyone seemed to be doing their job. We got four holes dug today. It looks like we're going to have some nice bunkers when we get done with them.

We worked on our new bunker most of the day. We are going to fill old ammunition boxes with dirt and put them along the walls. That should keep the dirt from falling in on us and keep it from collapsing when we put the roof on. It's going to be a great bunker when it gets done.

Watanabe got a beautiful black eye from Parker today. I don't know exactly what happened, but Parker is one of those guys who doesn't take any shit from anybody. I guess Watanabe said something to him and Parker just decked him. I'm going to stay out of it. There's no sense trying to make them apologize to each other. They'll deal with it. We're just like a family here. Brothers get mad at each other, and ten minutes later it's all forgotten. I think that's the way it's going to be with Parker and Watanabe.

Shortround is having a little trouble. I don't know exactly what it is. I guess I'll have to sit down and talk to him. I've had a couple of complaints from the other guys about how he's been acting, so we have to spend some time talking to him.

Puff was working out hot and heavy just up northwest of us today. I don't know what he was shooting at, but he worked hard during the day, and even into the night, so there must be some gooks up there. Intelligence isn't always right, but by the way Puff was working out, the gooks may be getting close enough to hit us. Tonight would be a good night. It's dark and nasty out there. I know these damn gooks like this weather. They're used to it, and we're not.

We had another C-123 in today. It took a hit with some shrapnel. I guess they couldn't get it fixed; it's still sitting over there. Hopefully it will be out of here tomorrow. Those C-123s are damn good lift planes, but seems like every time one comes in here, they end up getting in trouble. Hopefully they'll get it fixed and get it out of here. I don't like those things sitting over there, because it gives the gooks more incentive to fire something in on us.

I can't wait until we get this new bunker done. I think it will withstand a direct hit when it's done. For tonight I'll sleep in the old one.

March 7

Quiet night, the LPs and everyone seemed cool. We didn't have any patrols out, so everything seemed to be alright.

Lt. Asmus [Stewart A., 0103324], Henry, Deschaine, and I worked on our new bunker. It's going to be really outstanding when we get it done. It's going to be the best bunker on the line. Deschaine and I went over to the air strip today and stole thirty pieces of runway matting. They are three inches by ten inches by twelve feet. What we're going to do, once we get the ammunition boxes filled to make the walls, is lay these across the top of it and then cover it with dirt. I think we'll have an outstanding bunker. We almost got caught getting the matting, though. Some airwinger was coming over toward us, and we had the matting with us. Deschaine just said we were supposed to pick this stuff up, and he didn't question us, so we skated.

The C-123 that was shot up yesterday took a direct hit today. So that's the end of it. That's number four junk plane we've got sitting out there. It's the fourth plane to get blown up on the runway.

I will sleep in the old bunker tonight, but not for too much longer.

March 8

We had quite a night. There was an awful lot of incoming during the night. We've had more and more incoming each day. It's mostly artillery. Somebody said that out near Co Roc, they've dug tunnels back inside the hill and the artillery pieces are sitting back inside. They just push them out, fire a few rounds, and pull them back in. Even the B-52s can't seem to knock them out. That would be a good operation for us. I'd love to take our troops out and try to take that hill.

I just kind of fooled around the area today and worked on the new bunker. It's going to be great by the time it gets done.

I found out about PFC Mead today. He had gotten wounded a couple days ago and was down at the hospital. He was on a C-123, along with 43 other guys and four crew members, that was shot down about five miles south of here. We heard about it yesterday, but nobody really knew for sure. That's too bad. The kid was only in the company for five days before he got wounded the first time. He went to the hospital and was on his way back when he got shot down. He was in the country for 22 days. It's really sad. I didn't know Mead very well, but he seemed like a pretty good kid. That's the worst part about this damn war. Seems like every time you turn around, somebody you know is getting killed, and it hurts a lot.

I feel kind of blue tonight. Mead is part of it, I'm sure, but there is more to it than that. The constant incoming is getting on my nerves. You can be out in the open for about five minutes and it starts. You run for cover and stay down. I've noticed some of the other guys—staff NCOs and officers, as well as the troops—are getting pretty jumpy. Maybe we'll go out after the bastards and put a stop to all this shit.

Hopefully we'll get the new bunker squared away and I can sleep in it before too long.

March 9

Quiet night, didn't have many incoming. All the LPs did fine.

We just worked on the bunker all day. We put the last of the ammunition boxes in and laid the runway matting on top. I'm sleeping in here tonight. I think it's safer than the other one. It's probably not, but at least we've got our bunks squared away, so I'm going to sleep in here. Hopefully we won't take any direct hits. It's down low, so it would have to be a direct hit before I would get hurt. We set it up so we have a sleeping space and a living space. When it's done, we should be able to be in our bunk and not be bothered by the people in the living area. I can't wait until it's done.

March 10

I slept pretty well in the new bunker last night, and we worked on it today.

This job as platoon sergeant has its drawbacks. I have to stay on the troops, mainly on the squad leaders, to get anything done. There isn't that much to do. I could get it done by myself in one day, but I'm the supervisor now, so I make sure the job gets done. I guess I'll learn how to do it eventually, but right now I'm having a little trouble with it. I just can't seem to talk to the guys in a way they understand and not sound like I'm bitching at them. I've got to stay on them because the gunny stays on me. I think maybe I'll be OK with it after a while. I'll just continue to tell the squad leaders and stay on them to see that it gets done. The funny thing is you don't want to piss anybody off too bad. Here in the combat zone, if you piss somebody off, they just might blow your head off the next time you're on patrol, and that's the end of it. I know we have some squad leaders that feel that way, and we've got some Marines here who are pretty bad dudes. I worry about that kind of thing too. I laid the law down to the squad leaders at the meeting we had this morning. I told them everyone's got to do their job so I can do mine.

I'll sleep on it and see how things are tomorrow.

March 11

We had some trouble with the LPs last night. Puyol [James E., 2281697] and Luster [Clinton B., 2338693] were out there together last night. Maybe we shouldn't have put them out together, since they're such good friends. I think sometimes they get to fooling around out there and stop paying attention to what they're supposed to be doing. I had a talk with Puyol this morning, and he was supposed to come and see me before he went back out tonight. But he didn't show up. He doesn't seem like too bad of a kid, but we've got to get him to understand that he's got a responsibility to the platoon. I may have to take him to have a talk with gunny. The gunny has more experience at this kind of thing than I do. I worry about these guys all the time. I worried about my squad when I was their squad leader, now as platoon sergeant I worry about the whole damn platoon, including Lt. Asmus. The Lt. does a great job as platoon commander, but it seems like it falls on the platoon sergeant's shoulders to talk to the troops and try to get things going.

Puyol is out on LP again tonight. I'm going to have the watch get me up every once in a while so I can check on him.

I'm sleeping in the new bunker.

March 12

I had some trouble with the LPs again last night. I can't understand it—these guys go out there and go to sleep. I know what it's like: you get out there in a bomb crater or up against a tree stump and you get tired and fall asleep. I don't know how to get them to take more responsibility for themselves. I just don't know what to do. I talked to the gunny about it, and he told me to just kick the shit out of them. I'm not sure I want to do that. At times I'd like to punch a few of them in the face, but I could end up getting my ass kicked. So I guess I won't do that. I don't know what it is, but I'm going to have to come up with something to keep them awake out there.

We got the dirt put back on top of our bunker today. It really looks like it's going to be solid. We got a table and our bunks into it, and it looks really nice. I think it looks great. We have the safest and the best-looking bunker out here on the lines. We also got the dirt put back on some of Shortround's bunkers, so the line is starting to shape up in places. The hooches we sleep in look pretty solid.

Corbett's squad has a patrol tomorrow. I don't know how far he is going out for sure yet, but it looks like he will be going out in front of our area. I wish him the best. They had a little practice today, and it looks like they know what they are doing, so they should be safe. The new bunker helps me sleep better.

March 13

I was up at 0600 this morning. The LPs did alright during the night. Nobody had any bitches this morning, so the day started out alright. Corbett's squad motored out at 0730. Everything went outstanding until they reached the dump road. Heim [Steven T., 2285993] had the point, and he hit a grenade trip wire. He got hit in the legs, feet, and arms. His flak jacket really protected his upper body, though. Knox [David, 2324142] was right behind him, and he got hit in the arm, but not too bad. Hall was behind Knox, and he got hit in the face; he will be OK. They couldn't tell if it was an ARVN setup or a Chicom set in by the NVA. Three guys were hurt, regardless. Heim is going to be out for a while, because he got the worst of it, but I don't think the other guys will be out too long. They all seemed to be taking it well. I know the ARVN set those trip wires out there, and I understand that it's protection for them, but the sons of bitches ought to let us know where they are before we go out on patrols.

I had early watch tonight and the LPs had some movement out in front of bunker 39, so maybe the gooks are moving in. We told the LPs to watch real close. I couldn't do anything but keep talking to them. I stayed on the radio with them for about an hour, and the movement finally stopped. I told Corbett if the movement starts again to wake me up. I don't think I will sleep very well anyway.

March 14

Actually, the night turned out to be pretty quiet, even if it didn't start out too well. We went on 100% at dark, and we were on it until 2345. I went to sleep about 0030 and slept through the rest of the night. I guess we had about ten incoming.

I had a talk with the gunny and we decided to send four guys out on LPs. We started out with one, went to two right away. So maybe if we send out four on each LP we will be alright. What we are going to do is allow two to sleep and two to stay awake. Then they will switch. They will then stay out all night instead of only half the night. Maybe that will work out better. We had to come up with something to keep the guys awake out there.

Hall and Knox came back to the platoon today, but they kept Heim up in BAS. I think he will be up there a few more days anyway.

Bravo Company had one KIA and three WIAs. The platoon was outside the wire someplace.

We finished the inside of our bunker today and it looks really good. I hung my West Virginia flag up, and of course all the guys bitched about that, but I didn't care. I had a bunch of *Playboy* pictures, so we hung them up too. The guys didn't complain about them.

We had some real close air strikes today. The gooks must be coming in real close. The air strikes were so close you could see the faces of the pilots flying the planes.

I held a real quick rifle inspection today. I wanted to see if the troops were taking care of their weapons. Fox had a round in his chamber. I chewed his ass pretty good about it. I know they want to be ready to go if the shit hits and the gooks hit the wire, so they can keep their magazines in but not put a round in the chamber even with the rifle on safe. Burns, [Terry M., 2380976] had his rifle off safe, but at least he didn't have a round in the chamber. He said he didn't realize it. He said he didn't even think about checking it. Everyone else seemed to be OK. I know the guys want to be ready to fight but I told them we have to be safe too. We don't want any accidents. I don't want to see anybody killed by our own guys.

I'm going to sleep in our outstandingly safe new bunker tonight. I think I will sleep very well.

March 15

We had a very busy night. We went on 100% two or three different times. As soon as we would come off 100%, one of the LPs would see something or somebody would throw a grenade and we would be back up again. I only got about two hours' sleep all night.

Lt. Asmus and Henry had to leave the first thing this morning. I image it was some kind of company meeting, and they were gone most of the day. So I was in charge all day.

Bravo picked up the sound of a tank on a tipsy. It was something I didn't know we even had on the base. I guess it picks up sounds through the earth. We never saw anything of the tank. I still think there are tanks in the area. As steep as most of the hills are around here, they aren't going to be running them up and down the hill trails, but they could run them over some of the hills. It would be real easy for them to travel over the lower trails and roads, but next to impossible on the high hills.

I went up to BAS to see Heim, and he is doing good. He'll probably be up there another ten days to two weeks. He seemed to be pretty happy. We were talking about safe bunkers, and the ones they are in are really safe. I'm sure he will be OK in a few days.

3/26 lost a starlight scope. The word is it was captured, but I bet they just lost it. I'll bet they were out on patrol someplace and whoever was in charge of it laid it down and when they moved out they left it there. I guess the battalion commander was really pissed about it. One of the advantages we had was being able to see the gooks at night when they couldn't see us. Now if they have the starlight scope, they are going to be able to see us at night too. It kind of pissed me off too. They could use the thing to look at the Gray Alpha lines and shoot me right in the head.

I had watch from 1100 until 0020. It's nice to have the early watch, because you don't get wakened in the middle of the night. I can finally get some sleep.

March 16

It wasn't too bad of a night. I slept for a while. I didn't have a watch, so it wasn't too bad for me. I slept pretty well.

We did have some real close air strikes. One of the LPs, Hollier, (full name and service number not available) got hit with a piece of shrapnel from one of the bombs. Burns went out to take his place. I don't know if the gooks are in that close or if they are just trying to keep them pushed back. The air strikes were within 50 meters of the wire. The guys were saying you could hear pieces of shrapnel flying over the line every once in a while. It was too close. Luckily, the LP wasn't hurt too bad. I guess he got some shrapnel in his shoulder and one of his hands. Other than that he wasn't too bad.

I just fooled around most of the day and worked on the bunker a little bit. We just straightened a few things up.

I heard they had a few gooks in the trench line out in front of the ARVN lines. One of the ARVN got hit when the gooks tried to come through the wire. I guess the gooks know where the ARVN are and they think they can get through there easier than they can through 3/26 or our lines. They said the gooks were in their trench lines and that's pretty scary when they get through the wire that far. They would have some trouble getting through our concertina and tanglefoot, but still, if they can get through the ARVN lines, they may take a shot at getting through ours.

They brought in a whole lot of mail today. It was really nice. I got some letters from home and from some other people I don't know. I think everyone in the platoon received some mail, and it's great to see all the guys happy for a few minutes anyway. I went up to get it and they had two big bags just for our company. It was really nice to get the mail from home. You know, you don't really appreciate home like the guys do when they get some mail from home. It's been almost three weeks since we've had any mail. I can understand that it's hard to get it in here now. They don't want to just dump it out of a plane and hope that it lands someplace inside the wire. The plane that came in last night just hit the runway and opened a parachute and the chute drug the stuff out the back of the plane. It was a C-130. As soon as the stuff was out the back, the pilot hit the gas and it started climbing and kept right on going. We were lucky to get mail, and we appreciate the guys that brought it in.

Everyone seems to be doing good back home. It really makes me feel good to find out there aren't any problems back home.

It's time to hit the rack.

March 17

I slept pretty well until about 0200. Then we went on 100% for about two hours. Someone heard or spotted eight tanks. I guess they must have spotted them and figured out where they were. They were someplace down near Khe Sanh Ville. When it's real quiet at night you can hear them, and last night I could hear them. When we were brought up 100%, the guys said they were out there. I never saw them.

I had some trouble with DeSilva (Berry, 2280797). He doesn't want to follow orders very well. I'm not sweating it too much; he is leaving for CAC tomorrow. So I'm not going to worry about him too much.

I just fooled around the bunker today and didn't do much. There wasn't anything to do.

The ARVN got hit pretty hard this morning. The gooks are really working on that section of the lines which is about 400 meters from us. I don't know if they think that is a weak spot in the lines or what. There was no mention of any gooks getting through this time. We wouldn't know the difference if they came through here. If the North Vietnamese regulars didn't have their uniforms on, most Americans wouldn't know whether they were ARVN or North Vietnamese. So that gets kind of scary too. I guess we would shoot first and ask questions later.

We picked up three new guys today. They are Sequra [Michael T., 2384417], Martinez [Bernard, 2155579], and Sanchez [Carlos, 2346604]. They are pretty young, pretty inexperienced, and just right out of basic training. So I will try to work them in slowly. I'm going to put two of them in Corbett's squad. Doug does a good job of breaking in new troops. I don't know what we will do with the other guy, but I will put him someplace. Hopefully we can keep them alive for a few weeks. The new guys were telling us that there are a lot of people back in the world that don't think we should be here. I will go along with that. They said there are protests almost every day on television. I told them we don't have a choice. We are Marines and our country sent us here so we must make the best of it. If some sorry ass has a problem with what I'm doing over here, have him bring his sorry ass over here and see if he can do a better job.

I wonder how long these new guys will last.

I'm going to sleep.

March 18

What a night! I didn't get more than a half hour of sleep all night long. I hit the rack about 2000 hours and was back up at 2030 for about an hour. We thought for sure we were going to get hit. We were finally going to get some action. We could just feel the gooks moving our way. You know, it's just the sensation that you have. You can't see them, but you can smell them. Sometimes when the wind is just right, you can smell them. I just knew they were coming in. I could just feel it. But they never showed up. Maybe tomorrow we'll see the bastards.

I hit the rack at 2330, and Gunny Ross [Robert, 1233091] got me up at 0100 to shoot a few rounds over the LPs' heads to wake them up. He was really hot; I don't know why he was involved in it anyway, unless he was just down checking the lines and found out that they were sleeping. But I fired a couple rounds over their heads, and they got up. Puyol came back in a second time. The first time, he said he had to talk to Corbett. He was really upset and scared. You know, I understand it is tough being out there on an LP, especially when the gooks are this close. They can walk right past you. They can walk right up on you and maybe end up killing you before you realize they are there. He was pretty upset about it, but I made him go back out anyway. I feel for him, but we all have to do our job.

I couldn't go back to sleep, and it was just as well. We went on 100% at 0430. We were back out in the trench again. You know, it just seems like it's imminent (that's the word we hear from intelligence all the time). I do believe they will hit us full force before long. It's just a matter of time. I hope I'm awake when the shit happens.

I was really tired all day. Every time I would try to lie down and get some sleep, someone else would want me.

I have to do something about these LPs. We have been putting them out in groups of two or four and try to keep one of them awake at all times, but it just doesn't seem to work. Every night it seems like someone is going asleep and we can't make radio contact with them. When the gooks are this close, you think that maybe they are all dead, so the squad leaders have to crawl out there and find them and that is a real scare too. When you crawl right up on them you don't know if they are going to shoot you when they wake up and think you are a gook. It's really frightening. I just don't know what to do about it. I tried to talk to the gunny and top about it and they both just chewed my ass about it. The think I should just kick the kids' asses. I asked them if they had some magical cure to stop it or what they would do if they were the platoon sergeant. So far they haven't been able to tell me anything I didn't already know. I have to do something about it and soon. I can't have these guys going to sleep on LPs every night. One of these nights the gooks are going to hit us and we won't know it in time because the damn LPs are asleep.

I'm so fucking tired I can't see straight. I'm going to hit the rack and hope the squad leaders will keep the LPs awake.

March 19

It wasn't too bad of a night. I finally got some sleep. I was really tired last night. I think everybody knew it, so they left me alone.

We had several incoming rounds last night. They fired them in at night, which was kind of a surprise. They seem to keep firing during the daytime when we are up moving around. We have had a few rounds at night, but nothing like last night.

2nd Platoon came down to our lines and fired a few rounds to check their rifles. They just messed things up all over the place. They just didn't care. They left spent cartridges lying all around. We had this 55-gallon can of mo-gas out in front of our lines that we were saving to light up the place if the gooks ever did hit us. Some idiot shot a hole in it and caught it on fire. When it cooled down we went out and got the can out of there. That was real scary, going out through the lines in the daylight. We found another can, and we are going to try to find some gas to put in it.

I finally got the top and gunny off my ass. I told them that when I send the LPs out from now on they are going to key the handset every 15 minutes, hopefully. Not a real great idea, nothing real fancy, but maybe that will keep them awake. If they key the handset I will know they are awake and I won't have to worry about them so much. Plus I will know they are still alive. The gunny and top seemed to think that at least it is something worth trying. I hope it works. We tried it with the group that went out tonight, and they were keying the handset sometimes. I bet no one out there has a watch they can read.

Fuck it, I'm going to go to sleep.

March 20

The LPs didn't go to sleep last night. So maybe the idea worked. At least they were awake most of the night. They didn't key the handset every 15 minutes but close to it.

I lost a good buddy today, Vantassell [James, 2303037]. It was real sad. We used to be really tight when we were hitting the bush a lot. He was a pretty cool dude. He didn't have his flak gear on and really got it bad. The doctors don't give him much of a chance. Even if he does live, they said that he will probably be a vegetable. I just gave him hell yesterday for not wearing the damn gear. I really liked him, and the chances are he is not going to make it. I'm really going to miss the big bitching lug. He was a really great Marine.

I went up to medevac this afternoon to see if Jim was still there, but they wouldn't let me in to see him, so I don't know what kind of shape he's in. I mean, he must have been torn up pretty bad. I hope his parents can live with it. I just hope to God that he goes to heaven.

Boltz, David, (service number not available) was the other guy. I didn't know him too well. They said that he took it pretty bad too. I don't know if he'll make it or not.

I had to bust a couple of guys' asses again today for not wearing their gear. You know, these guys don't seem to understand. I mean it's heavy, it's bulky, and it's as hot as hell, but at least it will keep you alive. You know, I just can't understand it. These guys need to wear this stuff, and that's my job to bust their ass about it. I got on the squad leaders about it too. I told them that if they didn't start keeping people in their flak gear when they're out here messing around, filling sandbags or whatever they are doing, that we are going to have to do something about it.

I don't know; things are getting real tense here. Here we are in a defensive position all the time. We don't get a chance to go out and do anything. Bravo Company has a patrol tomorrow. Man, I wish we had gotten that patrol. I would like to take this platoon out and get them doing something. We are really getting tense. You know we are starting to get on each other's nerves. We were trained to fight, not sit back in this hole and do nothing.

Just let me go to sleep and get one more day over with.

March 21

The LPs did fine last night. I was on watch for a while, and every 15 minutes they keyed the handset. They seem to be doing a lot better.

Bravo's patrol went off pretty well. They had four WIAs; one by our own 60 mm mortars. Some of the mortar guys up here don't pay much attention to what they are doing. I think we all are going crazy. They dropped a 60 right on top of the patrol. One WIA was from the ARVN. I guess the ARVN were firing 81s and dropped one down on them. One guy tripped a booby trap. I don't know what happened to the other guy. The booby trap was an M-26; they think it was from one of Bravo's dead.

We really put out some firepower in support of Bravo Company. That is the first time I have seen Khe Sanh Combat Base and the other bases in the area put out that kind of firepower in support of anyone. We had 60s, 81s, 105s, and 155s all working out. We were really rocking. We even had the 106 recoilless rifles into it. We even had the 175s from Camp Carroll firing; when you hear those babies coming over, they sound like a train. If nothing else, at least we shook the gooks up a little bit today. Maybe they will be a little hesitant to come roaring in here now that they see what kind of firepower we have. I wonder how many rounds we have left. We haven't been resupplied with ammunition for a while, so we could be getting low on ammunition. I just watched what Bravo Company was doing during their patrol. I have the late watch, so I won't sleep.

March 22

The LPs are still doing well, so my idea seems to be working. I just fooled around the area today. I played chess with Henry and checkers with Shortround. It was kind of relaxing, kind of a real quiet day.

Things were pretty quiet until about 2015. All hell broke loose. I was just getting ready to try and clean up a little bit. We had some extra water today, so I thought maybe I'd wash my face. I wasn't going to worry about shaving, just try to clean up a little. We all stink like goats around here. The gooks hit us with everything they had. There was 179 artillery and some big rockets, probably 140 mm. It lasted about an hour. We did have a few incoming and some light artillery after that. They just really blanketed us. We were all out in the trenches, and our first thought was "Here it comes. The gooks are going to blast us for a while and then hit the lines." But so far, I haven't heard anything.

Taylor from second squad got hit in the back of the head, and he's really lucky. He is still alive. They said he may have to have brain surgery. I don't really know what kind of shape he's in. But it would have killed him for sure if he hadn't had his helmet on. So maybe some of the guys will begin to realize that they have got to wear their helmet and gear all the time. I don't know what kind of shape the guy's in, but I will go up in the morning and see what I can find out.

Van is still in critical condition. They haven't been able to medevac him out yet. Hopefully they are able to keep the blood supply up and the other things the doctors need up there. I'll go up and see Van tomorrow if they will let me in to see him and check on Taylor.

We had one hell of an evening. I hope they don't keep this shit up all night. I would like to get some sleep.

March 23

I hit the rack at 2330 and went right to sleep, but I was back up at 0215 for 100%. Intelligence told us that the NVA were going to hit us at 0300, but you know how that goes. I don't think the intelligence boys have any idea what the hell is going on. The gooks didn't show up at 0300 anyway.

We did have a really heavy artillery attack. The gooks were firing in what we thought were the biggest yet, probably from Hill 179. I can't believe we don't know where they are firing from. You would think anyone could find those damn guns and put them out of commission. Someone said they were coming from out around Hill 471. I don't think anyone knows where they are firing from, but they are sure knocking the hell out of us. It seemed like the biggest artillery rounds we have had so far, so maybe they are different guns and bigger guns. I don't know if they are 179 mm or not.

As far as I know, we didn't have any wounded. Luckily, none of them hit real close to us. Of course we are out here on the lines and most of the rounds hit back toward main side.

Charlie Company got hit and five guys got killed. I imagine they were the company commander and service personnel. I didn't go over to see, and I'm not going to. I don't need to see any more shit like that. We heard the bunker took a direct hit.

We knocked off 100% at "stand to." I have been sleeping most of the day and I'm still tired and really tense. Night after night, intelligence keeps telling us the gooks are going to hit us and they don't. It's like the little kid crying "wolf" all the time. One of these nights they are going to hit us and we won't believe it and won't be prepared.

I'm going to do my best to keep the troops ready and keep them awake. I will keep them out there doing what they are supposed to do.

So far tonight the LPs have been good. I have the watch at 0300, so we will just have to wait and see what happens.

March 24

It was a pretty quiet night. The LPs are doing pretty good now. We haven't had much incoming all day.

Henry and Henkel took off today. I hope they have a nice R&R. Hopefully they will bring us back some booze or something we can have some fun with.

I worked on Knox's tape recorder today. I have been sending tapes home, and I would like to continue doing that but my tape recorder went bad. So I tried to fix Knox's but I don't think it's going to work.

Gunny Ross came down and gave me a shipping-over lecture. (Sign up for four more years.) You know, it didn't sound too bad. I'm due to get out when I leave Nam, so in a few more months it will be time to get out. It sounded pretty good, and I talked to him about shipping over for embassy duty. That's what I would really like to do. He wants me to give it some thought and talk to him in a couple weeks. I'll probably do that.

We had a really hard rain today. It just soaked us. It was like it rained all day and just kept raining into the night.

The LPs were going out and they tripped the wire to the 55 gallons of mo-gas we had put outside the wire. It was kind of funny watching them dive for cover when it went off. There was so much light you could see all around the place. They ended up crawling out in all that mud. It was not a pretty sight.

Most of the guys are doing pretty good. I had a little trouble with Dennis today, but I think we have that squared away. I'm proud of all the guys; they work hard even with all the incoming and the shit that goes on around here.

It's time to hit the rack.

March 25

The LPs messed up last night. When I got up to go on watch at 0300 they were asleep. I had put Puyol in charge. This is something else I have tried to keep them awake. I thought I would put one of the LPs in charge out there and kind of make him the leader and give him the responsibility of keeping everybody awake. So Puyol was in charge last night. It didn't seem to work very well. I don't know what happened to him; he just said he went to sleep. The next thing he knew, everybody was asleep. Watanabe, O'Neil [Michael J., 2385656], and Coleman [Charles, 2226164] were the other guys out there with him. Puyol is just about at the end of his rope. The other guys are going to hang him. I mean, he cannot stay awake out there on watch. I am afraid the CO is going to have him this time. He is a good kid; he really is a good kid and he tries hard. Maybe he is one of those guys who just can't stay awake at night. The gunny wanted to see him, so I took him over there and put in a few good words for him. I didn't hear what the gunny said, but I know he had a piece of his ass.

We got the word today to pack up. It looks like we are going to pull off these lines. Nobody knows where we are going. God, I hate to leave this bunker. We worked our butts off on this thing and it's really nice and safe. I really hate to leave it.

1/9 lost some guys while they were out on patrol. They left three bodies out in the bush. That's really terrible. You know, as Marines when guys get killed or wounded we never want to leave them out there. Let's just hope that the guys out there are still alive and we can find them and get them back in before the gooks find them. I saw 1/9 going through the lines. They went out through the wire and came back about two hours later. I knew as soon as I saw them coming back in they had gotten hit. You could see that look of fear on their faces. They didn't stop to talk; they motored right on through and back to their own area.

This may be my last night in my wonderful bunker. I'd better sleep well tonight. It may be a long time before I get to sleep in this kind of safety.

March 26

The LPs did a good job last night. No one seemed to go to sleep. I had the watch at 0400, and they were wide awake when I was out there. Everything seemed to be OK.

I packed some of my gear away today. I'm really going to miss that radio. It's nice to have even though we don't get a whole lot on it. We pick a station once in a while and get some music.

1/9 got hit when they went out today to pick up the KIAs. They took 5 KIAS and 15 WIAS. They went out to get those bodies they left out there yesterday. If they would have brought them in yesterday, look at the lives they would have saved. That's really stupid. I can't understand it; I mean, I know darn good and well that I'd never let my platoon pull out and leave somebody, even under fire. We would definitely bring our bodies in. They ended up getting 2 more KIAS today and 15 wounded. I don't know how bad they are, but they could be KIAs too. It was really stupid; I don't know why they did that.

Puyol got seven days' loss of pay for going to sleep on watch. That was just what the company commander gave him. They were going to take him before the battalion commander for "office hours," but they decided not to do it. Gunny told me that seven days' loss of pay wasn't a good idea. What's seven days' loss of pay going to do to you in this place? It's not like we have a lot of money and really want to spend it. There's nothing to spend it on anyway. Hopefully it will change him. Maybe he will realize that he has a lot of responsibilities out there on listening post.

Deschaine beat me playing checkers today. We have a little checker tournament going here. We decided to do that just to kind of pass the time. Deschaine beat me once and he beat the lieutenant twice, so I don't feel too bad about that. It gives us something to do. It is less dangerous that firing razor blades at each other, which is what we have been doing. The lieutenant doesn't like us to do that. He gets fired up; of course, I just know it's because he is a lieutenant and we are all enlisted people. What are you going to do? You can't play tiddly winks here. As I already said, you have to find some kind of game. I'm pretty good at shooting razor blades.

We didn't leave the lines today; one more night in our bunker. I really hate to leave this bunker.

March 27

The LPs did a good job last night. I didn't have the watch last night, so I didn't have to go out on the lines. Everybody told me that they stayed awake all night long. So that's a good sign.

I spent the day packing people's gear who are on R&R. I got all that stuff cleaned up and put away.

Verschage [Ray, 2395922] and Hempill [Garry,L. 2063752] got back off in-country. Verschage brought back two radios and a case of Pepsi for his squad, which is pretty nice of him. We each got a taste. That tasted pretty good—-first Pepsi I've had in a long time. Of course, it was warm, but who cares? It wasn't too bad.

Washington (Jeffrey, 2367114) didn't come back with them. I don't know why, but maybe he just couldn't get on the same chopper that they were on. He didn't show. So we will have to wait and see if he shows up tomorrow.

Deschaine got his first kill in Nam. He just killed an ant. It may be the only one he will get. I felt sorry for the little ant. Deschaine made a big deal out of it; he jumped up and down and stomped on it. It was really funny. It was a good laugh. That's something that we haven't done too much of around here lately. There's nothing like a good laugh to help lower the tension.

We have four guys living in this bunker together. We all get along pretty well, but still there is some tension every once in a while.

I borrowed a camera off Lieutenant Simpson, and Doc Whitehouse gave me five rolls of film, so I'm going to take some pictures around here—some pictures of the guys as they work on the wire and different things. It's something to do to keep some memories of this place, although there are not a lot of good memories. Maybe some pictures will make it a little better.

We didn't move off the lines today, maybe tomorrow.

March 28

I took the LPs out and set them in tonight. I wanted to know exactly where there were. I thought maybe that would give me a little better idea what it's like out there. They set in inside a bomb crater that was pretty straight on one side, which gave them some cover, so they were pretty safe. The crater was just deep enough that you could be safe and still see out of it. It gave them a pretty good view of the terrain. It was a hairy trip. I still don't know how the guys go to sleep out there. I don't think I could go to sleep at all. I spent about an hour out there with them. It was pretty hairy. I wouldn't want to do that all the time. I stood LP duty up on the hills, but the gooks weren't as close as they are now.

I went to the BAS today to check on my health records and make sure I was up to date on all my shots. That was something the gunny told me I had to do, so I went and did it. They have everybody medevaced from my platoon. I haven't heard about Van for a while, so I don't know if he is alive or not. All the guys that were in serious condition got medevaced out. This morning the gooks had a body hanging from a tree out in front of us. We think it was a Marine, probably from Bravo Company. They couldn't tell for sure from this distance. Looking through binoculars, it looked like an American. They had him hung with a rope around his neck and his dick cut off and stuck in his mouth. It really fired us all up. We wanted to go out there and cut him down. We had several guys firing at the tree. Finally, we dropped an 81 mm mortar on the edge of the tree and that knocked it over. So at least we didn't have to look at him anymore. It was really a discouraging sight for all of us. I know it really bothered me.

Bravo Company is going to go out and try to recover some of the bodies, maybe tomorrow. I sat in on the preparation meeting, and if they run it like they planned, they don't stand a chance. They are just going to walk out there in columns. They will probably walk into an ambush like they did the last time. I really hope they give it some more thought before they go out there.

I'm thinking about shipping over again. I talked to the gunny again today. I'm going to go talk to the top tomorrow. It sounds like a good deal. I don't see myself doing anything else anymore. Here I am in combat, and I like it. I like being here, and I like what I'm doing. I don't like killing people, but it is one of the things you have to do, I guess. There is a lot of responsibility for the lives of others in this situation. I always wanted to be a teacher, but I don't know if I could work in a classroom after doing all this.

We are going down to man Bravo lines tomorrow so they can get some sleep before they go out on patrol. I sent a couple guys down there tonight to watch the guns. We will be down there on their line only a couple nights, I hope. I hope their lines are as good as ours.

I hope I get some sleep tonight.

March 29

It was a pretty quiet night. The LPs seemed to do OK. There wasn't any action at all. There wasn't even any incoming.

I found out that Captain Hughes [Edward J.] wrote me up for meritorious sergeant; that made me feel good. I guess he thinks I'm doing a pretty good job, or at least somebody does. It has to go to Division to be approved. I hope it gets back quick. Being a corporal and being a platoon sergeant doesn't draw any respect from some people. If I make sergeant I will be really happy.

I took Shortround and his squad down to Bravo lines today. The Bravo guys didn't look like they were up for a fight. Our guys here in Delta Company are raring to go. We would go out there in a heartbeat. Bravo just didn't seem like they were ready for it. The guys were anxious about going out, and I can understand that. Anybody is going to be anxious about out there, but they were going out to get the bodies of their buddies. As a matter of fact, I think if some of them could find a way out of going, they would have done it. With that kind of attitude I don't think they will do real well out there.

I'm the sole man in charge of my men here on Bravo lines. I have a lot of responsibility. I can make any kind of decision I want, and I hope I will make all the right ones and keep my guys alive. I won't stop worrying about the guys.

March 30

It was pretty quiet all night. We didn't have to put out any LPs down here. So I don't know how things went up on our lines, but things were pretty quiet here.

Bravo Company pulled out of their lines at 0500. They left the lines out in front of FOB at 0600. They got out about 100 meters when they first got hit. It was foggy, so I really couldn't see what was going on. We could hear plenty of rifle fire. We found out later that Bravo hit an NVA bunker complex. It was really well secured and well built in. They got across about half the bunkers and couldn't make it to their objective. I heard later the troops moved under heavy mortar fire and grenades. I don't know how many guys they had wounded yet. From what I understand, they had 9 KIAs and figured about 48 WIAs. They were able to get two bodies. They did get 6 confirmed, they said. They think they may have killed as many as 115 NVA. They found what they think was some kind of listening device. They brought that in to company headquarters today.

They said that the bunkers were unbelievable. They are really built up, well-built, well-constructed. They had good solid roofs on them. It looked like the gooks had moved in there and they are going to be there for a while.

It was funny that they should send Bravo Company out. I understand why they did it, I guess. Bravo Company had taken such an ass kicking out there a couple of weeks ago, they wanted to give them a chance to redeem themselves. I watched them leave here, and I didn't think that they would do a very good job. I just wondered what would have happened if Delta Company had gone out there. I can't guarantee we would have done any better, but we would like to try.

I'm back in my own bunker tonight, so I'm going to sleep better, I'm sure.

March 31

It was a pretty quiet night. There wasn't much happening. Bravo did a pretty good job, I guess, overall. They brought back some AK-47s and some other things. They put those on display and I went down to take a look at them. They seem like they did a pretty good job. They did lose some guys, but, you know, that is going to happen. I guess when you go out and get in combat like this and get in firefights, you are going to lose some guys. They did get two of their bodies back from the ambush.

I am not really feeling too well today. I have a cold and can't seem to shake it. It didn't help sleeping on the ground in that bunker on Bravo lines the other night. But I'll live with it.

Shortround has a patrol tomorrow. It is going to go about 1,000 meters off the south end of the runway. I hope he does OK.

I feel like shit tonight.

April 1

I really messed up last night. I kind of fooled around talking to the guys, and I didn't get but four hours of sleep. I was up because the LPs were messing around out there. I don't think they were asleep, but I don't know what they were doing. They didn't hear anything, or they didn't say they heard anything. We just couldn't make contact with them. When they came in, they said they didn't hear us. I should have gone out to check on them. I will if it ever happens again.

Shortround jumped off at 0830. He didn't go out earlier because of the fog. He went out off the south end of the runway and swept about 100 meters directly across in front of our lines. He didn't do too bad of a job. He didn't cover all the area in front of bunker 37 to the dump road, but he got it done. Like he said when he came back in, it was scary as hell out there. He is a pretty good squad leader. He did a good job out there today. It is scary. His self-confidence has really come up since I first met him. I think part of that is being a squad leader, and he has responsibility. He is taking charge and doing a good job.

I had to attend a class today on starlight scopes. We got them zeroed in on our M-16s, so I think that will really help us. They are really the neatest thing in the world. I don't care how dark it is, you just point it out there. Somehow it takes every bit of starlight that is out there and makes it so that you can really see. Things look kind of fuzzy, but you can really see anything that is out in front of you. Each squad has got one now. Hopefully, they will hang on to them and won't lose them. They are really going to help us out, I think, as far as seeing things at night.

We got the word today that a bunch of Allied troops, probably most of them from the Army, jumped off someplace down south. I don't know if it was down around Phu Bai or where it was (someplace down Highway 9). They are going to move in toward Khe Sanh. We know that we are surrounded here, and we have taken a lot of shit. I guess these guys will liberate us. It makes me feel good to know that this shit might be over soon.

April 2

I sat up and played poker with Myers, (full name and service number not available) Pix, [Pixley, Glenn E., 2286650], and Lt. Asmus until midnight. I was supposed to get up for watch at 0400. They came in and woke me, and I didn't get up. I am not going to let that happen again. I mean, that is a hell of good thing to show the troops. Here I am, the man that is ripping everybody else's ass for not getting up and doing what they are supposed to do, like staying awake all night on watch, and look what I did. Someone came in and woke me up; I knew I was awake. I thought, "I will lay here for a second," and the next thing I knew, it was already 0600. I am not going to let that happen again.

I went over to the Ponderosa and took a shower today. The first shower I have had in quite a while. I didn't know that they had water over there. When I found out, I went over and took a shower. It really felt good. It was the first shower I have had in months. Out here we have washed our faces a few times, but this is the first time I really got to wash all over. t. Asmus, Shortround, Corbett, and myself had a little contest with M-79s today. I didn't do too bad; I surprised myself. It was the first time I had fired one in a while, but I didn't do too bad. I couldn't beat Corbett. Corbett is really outstanding with an M-79. Of course, he packs one all the time. Wherever he goes, he has been carrying it and firing it for quite a while now. I will tell you what, Corbett can knock an ant off an elephant's ass at 50 meters. He is really good with it. The lieutenant is not bad either, but he is not anywhere as good as Corbett.

The lieutenant and I had a little talk with Shortround today. We told him we were very proud of what he had done yesterday. And the fact that he showed a lot of balls out there with those guys. We did mention casually that he didn't go across bunker 37 and out to the dump road, but we didn't make a big deal out of it. We are really trying to make him feel good about himself. He is a good Marine. He does a good job and works hard at it. We told him that we were really proud of what he had done.

I got the word late tonight that we are going to have a patrol coming up. We don't know exactly when yet. They want Delta Company to go out toward where Bravo Company went and take the trenches in front of the ARVN lines. It looks like the kind of patrol that we are looking for. We are hoping that we can get some action out there. Every guy that I have talked to about it is really excited. I think we are all a little nervous, but we are tired of sitting in these damned trenches and doing nothing.

I got the word, too, that the troops are moving north, moving a little closer every day. They think that they will be up to the bridge tomorrow. I hope we get to take those gook bunkers before they get here and they do it. We have been sitting inside this wire too long. I'm ready to take it to those bastards.

April 3

The ARVN got hit about 2000 tonight. It didn't seem to be too bad. They said the gooks were rushing the lines but didn't get through the wire.

I got the word on a couple company-sized patrols in the works. I hope at least one of them comes off. One of them is to move out through the FOB gate and down the road to take what they think is a gook Battalion CP and a company-sized mortar position. Two of our platoons and Alpha One will move through first. Then two platoons of Bravo Company are to hold a police call. The other platoon will be company sized. Our two platoons and Alpha One will be moving down the dump road at 2300 hours. We will set in by 2400 and be ready to move across in front of the ARVN lines at 0001. I'm not really keen about fighting at night, but we will fire flares and stuff so it shouldn't be too hard to see. Of course if I can see them I guess they can see me, oh shit. There is nothing definite yet. They have to wait on Battalion and Regiment to give us the OK. I know the guys are really anxious to get out there. They would like to get out and do something, not just sit behind the lines. These kinds of patrols, either one of them, would be good. I will take either one just to get my guys out of here and do something else for a while. I went down to the ARVN lines to take a look out in front of them. Things are really blown up out there. You wouldn't believe the holes from our own artillery, mortars, and air strikes. There are no trees at all. It is all blown to hell. They say there are trenches out there also and gooks down in bunkers. I can't wait. I know the gooks can dig deep and build good trenches. It should be a good patrol. It will be a good operation for us.

    I couldn't believe the ARVN lines. They are a mess. Those guys don't take care of anything. There was one guy standing up on one bunker firing an M-60 machine gun. It looked like he was playing John Wayne or something. I was told they do it all the time.

    I had a little talk with Heim today. His attitude has kind of fallen apart. He doesn't want to listen to his squad leader and doesn't seem to want to do much. Part of it, I'm sure, is the tension we all feel. He is a good kid, good soldier, and good Marine. I told him that he must follow orders if he likes it or not.

    We had the strangest thing happen about 1600 tonight. I was sitting in the door of my bunker and a plane flew over. No one knew what kind of plane it was. Deschaine thought it was a WWII plane. It was so low you could see the pilot's face. He was wearing an old leather-looking helmet. I couldn't tell if he was gook or not but we all agreed it probably was. We figured they were taking pictures of the base. They called the Marine Air Wing and they scrambled a couple jets. The jets flew over a few minutes later, but the plane was long gone. Someone said it look like a B-29, maybe a B-25. It could have been either, but I'm sure it was a WWII plane.

    I'm going to get some sleep and hope for a patrol soon.

April 4

The ARVN got hit early this morning. There didn't seem to be too much action, but the gooks are picking on the ARVN every night.

1/9 jumped off early. They took Hill 471, and it looked like it was an outstanding job. We could watch most of the action from bunker 39. We watched them move right up the hill. They didn't seem to have any contact at all. When they got almost to the top of the hill they really caught hell. We could see the gooks were right on top of the ridge and were firing down on them. They made it to the top though and had to fight their way down the other side. The word is they only took 3 KIAs and 30 WIAs. They were resupplied by 1930, so they should be in good shape for the night. It was quite a show; it reminded me of a John Wayne movie. We could see the troops moving up the hill zigging and zagging, trying to get through the grass. When they got to the top, they just moved into the gook trench lines and right over the top of the hill.

I just hung around the company CP today waiting for some scoop. I spent most of the afternoon up there and didn't hear a thing.

The air around Khe Sanh is really jumping. The Allied troops are all over the place. We see a lot of regular helicopters and some big crane helicopters. I saw one today with some kind of artillery piece hanging from it. I don't know where they were going with it but you could see them a long way off down to the south. The Allies are moving in from the south, southeast, east, northeast, and northwest. I heard a really funny story today. I guess it was really not funny, but to us Marines it was funny. They said that some Army outfit threw something at the 1st Marines today and they ended up in a firefight. Three Dogfaces were killed and no Marines were even wounded. I have often heard that the Marines and the Army don't get along very well, but to shoot each other, that's funny. I don't know the whole story, but I hope the Marines didn't do it intentionally.

We had a mortar attack today but the mortars were filled with papers. After the mortars went off we found these real little papers. When we unfolded them we found a message from the gooks written on them. They wanted us to surrender. The CO told us they are called Chieu Hoi messages, they will make good shit paper.

The way things are jumping around the base, I would say the siege of Khe Sanh is about over.

I bet I get a good night's sleep.

April 5

It was a pretty quiet night and there hasn't been much happening during the day. It looks like some of the gooks are pulling out. The 1st Air Cavalry is moving toward us, and it looks like they will probably be in Khe Sanh tomorrow. There are a whole bunch of Allied troops in the area.

We are getting ready for our patrol tomorrow. The way things look, it shouldn't be too bad. The troops are really up for it too. They have been sitting in these damn bunkers long enough. They are ready to go. We are all ready to go. I think we would like to go out and kill some of these bastards who have been causing us such heartache and killing our friends and people we know.

I did go to communion today. We haven't had any kind of church services here since the chaplain got killed. They flew the communion in by chopper, and I got called by the company commander to go over and pick it up. I decided I was going to gave communion to any guy that wanted it even if they weren't Catholic. I felt that if receiving communion made them feel better, God would be OK with it. The only non Catholics that wanted it were Lutherans. The Catholics and the Lutherans got communion, so we are ready to go.

I'll probably sleep pretty light tonight. I'm kind of like the kid before the big game. I'm nervous and excited and ready to go. I just want to get through this night and go out on patrol tomorrow.

The author March 1968

Khe Sanh Combat Base

John Huskey

Fox preparing for a patrol

Deschaine playing with a mortar

Bru Villagers at our dump

Bru Villagers going through our trash

Part of the map we used in the Khe Sanh area of operation.

MOVING TREES

Left to right: Shortround and unknown Marines laying wire

Dead NVA

Dead NVA at Graves Registrations

Hill 881

Chopper bringing hot chow to Hill 881
Christmas Day 1967

Unloading Christmas Dinner

Left to right: Author, Unknown, Green
Eating Christmas Dinner on Hill 881

Left to right: Huskey, Bender

Left to right: Knox, Corbett

Point man going through
wire off Hill 881

YOU ARE TOLD:

US war escalation in Vietnam, intensification of attacks on the Democratic Republic of Vietnam, shelling of the North by long-range guns positioned south of the 17th parallel — all this is aimed at protecting the lives of GIs in Vietnam.

BUT WHAT YOU ACTUALLY GET IS:

— More bloody fighting along Highway 9;

— More artillery pounding of your posts, gun emplacements and bases in Gio-linh, Dong-ha, Da-nang, etc.

— Consequently: More American casualties and more sorrow for American families.

For every step taken by Johnson in escalating and intensifying the war either in North or South Vietnam shall meet with deserved punishment.

FOR GIs IN VIETNAM

the only way to save their lives is to:

— Refuse to take part in mop-ups and rescue operations!

— Demand their immediate repatriation!

— Let themselves be captured by the Liberation forces! All prisoners will be given humane treatment.

Truyền đơn dành cho lính Mỹ

Chieu Hoi message fired into Khe Sanh April 4, 1968

MCNAMARA:

1963: "The major part of the US military task can be completed by the end of 1963".

1964: "...Excellent progress in the war. It might be necessary to send certain additional US personnel to Vietnam, but only to expend the training of Saigonese forces".

1965: "We have stopped losing the war".

7-1966, in Hawaii:
We believe we are gaining".

BUT THE TRUTH IS:

More GIs put out of action every year in Vietnam.

1964: nearly 2,000
1965: nearly 20,000
1966: over 100,000

1967: The first months of 1967 have seen the highest weekly casualty rates of US troops in the war. (US News and World Report — March 13, 1967).

What GIs get from Johnson, McNamara...:
Blandishments and lies!

What they lose in Vietnam:
Their blood and their lives!

Chieu Hoi message fired into Khe Sanh April 4, 1968

Fred Seada

Left to right: Lt. Asmus, unknown, Shortround, Heim

Napalm being dropped on NVA bunkers

Left to right: unknown, Webb, Lt Asmus,
Unknown, watching Bravo Company

Left to right: Unknown, Markum

Left to right: Purdy, Heim
Filling sand bags at Wonder Beach

Left to right: Heim, Corbett

April 6

I was up at 0400 and got the troops ready to move out at 0500. We moved out the FOB gate at about 0630. We were making our way in a column down the road. It was really kind of scary, but we just marched down the road and got on line at the road toward the Combined Action Company 3. Everything was pretty quiet up to that point. The fog was really bad so we couldn't see much. But when it started to get daylight, we moved on up ready to start the attack. The FO called for artillery, and they fired out in front of us, really too close. It hit right in front of us. It hit Dennis, [Mitchell 2207332), Manns [full name and service number not available), and Gogolowski [Gary, 2261700). Dennis and Gogolowski were not too bad, but Mans was hit pretty badly. Dennis got it in the leg. Corbett came up on him and jumped his ass before he knew he had been hit. I'm pretty sure he will be OK. We had to medevac him out. I got hit in the face with a piece of shrapnel. It stuck in my hard head. I got hit in the forehead with a pretty big chunk, and I just pulled it out. It didn't go in too far. It bled really bad, but it seemed to be OK. The blood ran down my face and into my shirt pockets. It ruined my cigarettes and got on my Chieu Hoi message. I didn't care about the message, but I hate smoking bloody cigarettes.

We moved toward the objective. The troops had a hard time staying on line. It was really hairy. We were shoulder to shoulder practically and moving out across the bunker complex. It was pretty hard; some guys were moving faster than others. We didn't see any NVA. We got to our first objective in about 5 minutes and set up a perimeter to wait for Bravo Company to move up. We got the word then that the NVA were moving toward us, but we didn't see anything. We started to move back, policing the area as we went.

We found two Bravo bodies in sad shape; they were really torn up. One was a face, and I thought, "I am going to dig down around in the dirt and see if I can find the whole head." All I could see was the face, and the eyelids were shut. As I dug down, I found that there was nothing there. It looked like a Halloween mask. I just gathered it up and put it in a bag the best that I could. I found another body that was really in bad shape. It was a Marine, and there was no head or neck and no arms and no lower body—just the upper torso. I took a notebook out of his pocket. He was probably a squad leader. I found a boot with a foot in it sticking out of the ground. When I tried to pull it out if the ground, it came apart at the ankle. The flesh was like jelly. It really smelled bad. We found parts of three other bodies and a lot of gear, both Marine and NVA. Bravo Company really walked into a bad situation out there. I don't know whose fault it was or who caused it or what it was, but there were a lot of guys killed there. We moved back through the FOB lines. We got back in at 1230. We had a few guys wounded by our own fire, but no KIAs. We didn't see one fucking gook.

There was quite a mess out there. I don't know if the gooks have just pulled back and left everything, but we didn't see anybody at all. So I don't know what is going on there. I do know it's been a hell of a good day for our side. Husky, Corbett, Shortround, Deschaine, Lieutenant Asmus, and I had a little drink to celebrate.

The ARVN ran a patrol out in front of their lines at the same time we were out, and they had a little contact. They said that they did capture two recoilless rifles, an anti-aircraft gun, a couple of 50 calibers, a lot of NVA gear, and some individual weapons. There is one thing about being out there today that I will never forget, and that is the smell. Maybe my nose is working overtime, but all of those bodies, both NVA and Americans, are just rotting away out there. We tried to pick up everything that we could, but unless you can see them, you can't get them. I got the stuff on my hands; I can still smell it now. I don't know; it is something that I will never forget. It was the most terrible thing that I have experienced since being in Vietnam.

From what I understand, they have been able to identify 17 of the bodies that we brought in today. We got parts of several others that they are going to try to put together and see what they can find. The surprising thing was, though, I didn't see any dog tags at all on any of the Marines. Of course, we didn't pick up any whole bodies, but I didn't hear of anybody finding any dog tags out there. One thing that is really bad is that there have been so many bombs and stuff dropped out there, and the dirt is kicked up and has covered up a whole bunch of them. They are just buried there. These guys are going to be missing in action, and I would be willing to bet that most of their bodies are lying out there right now. I don't know; it is sad. It is one of those things that you'll just never forget as long as you live.

April 7

It was a pretty quiet day. I went outside the base, down to the dump road. I brought in some Army troops so they could get water.

The gunny told me that I did get a Purple Heart yesterday when I got hit in the head with shrapnel. So a Purple Heart, it will be nice to wear that on my uniform. Of course, they say that you get a Purple Heart when you make a mistake. So I made my first mistake. Maybe I won't get it again.

The word is that we are getting ready to pull out on an operation tomorrow. I don't know exactly where we are going to go. The word is that we are going up through Leach Valley. They said that there are a couple of objectives that we are going to try to reach tomorrow. One is a group of NVA trenches and bunkers. I don't know what that is going to be like. I hope that it is not what Bravo Company got into outside the base here. We are supposed to be pulling out early, but I don't know exactly what time. We will be moving north up through Leach Valley.

1/9 got hit last night. It's surely surprising that not one round went off. They brought the bomb chasers in and found out that there wasn't a fuse in any of them. So they were really lucky.

It was a bad night for 2/26, though; they lost a whole platoon. I guess the gooks dropped some mortars right in the middle of the platoon area and wiped out the whole platoon. They were out north- west of us and they said that the mortars just massacred the whole group of them.

April 8

I was up at 0600 getting ready to move out. I had to have a good police call and got the squad leaders moving pretty well. I was the only platoon sergeant that didn't get his ass chewed. Then we ended up sitting around waiting until 1130 for the Army to get in. They are going to take over our lines and be here in Khe Sanh while we are out on patrol. What a deal the Army has; they come marching up through here and taking over the place like they own it. All of their gear is brought in by choppers. It must be nice; this is the 1st Air Cav. and they have a pretty good deal. We have to carry our stuff and they get it brought in when they get wherever they are going to be. They get it dumped off by the choppers.

We saddled up and got off the base at 1330. They loaded us all in Hueys and flew us out into Leach Valley, and I don't know exactly where we are. We are not too far from the base; we can still see it. I guess we are out about 3000 meters.

We set in about 100 meters from this hill that we went over. We just got on line and went up the hill. We didn't get any resistance at all going up. We didn't see anything.

Boy, it is hot. I couldn't believe the kind of shape that I am in. Just sitting around all these months and not really getting ourselves in physical shape has really hurt us. I know that my old high school football coaches, Dom Ameado and Dick Bryan, ought to be here right now to help us get back in shape. I know they could get us in shape to play football. Right now not one of us is in good shape. We are all puffing and really sucking air.

We got to the top of the hill just before the rain hit. I got my poncho out and built myself a little hooch. I was in out of the rain by the time that it hit. The lieutenant, Fox, and Deschaine got soaked. I did help the lieutenant and Fox get one up, though, so they could at least get in out of the rain a little bit. We no more than got the hooches set up and got everybody in out of the rain when it stopped. The clouds kind of blew over and it really cleared up nice. We couldn't build any fires so we had to eat cold chow. But cold C-rations aren't the worst thing in the world. I still like my ham and lima beans. I am willing to trade anybody for those. I had the second watch, and nothing really serious happened. We had a little movement out by the LPs, but they didn't seem to be worrying too much about it, so I'm not either. The moon came out real bright, and it was really pretty, really quiet. You could hear a lot. You could hear things moving. It reminded me of home.

This place smells of NVA. One thing that has happened to me since I have been here, I have developed a really strong sense of smell. Maybe it is the animal instinct coming out in me. I can smell them, and the other guys can smell them too. That's probably why the smell of the dead bodies got to me so badly.

It's really light out tonight. Somebody is getting some action down near Khe Sanh Ville. I can hear the rifle fire.

April 9

I didn't get a whole lot of sleep last night. It seemed like every time I would go to sleep, the radio watch would wake me up to tell me that the LPs had movement. The LPs said that they saw four NVA moving across their front. They didn't really have any trouble though. So I didn't get a whole lot of sleep.

I was up at 0600. We had a platoon-sized patrol out in front of our area. We just moved out from the east side and moved around across the north side of the area and back in. We found three NVA bodies and about fifty 61 mm mortars and a whole bunch of AK-47s. They hadn't been lying out there too long. All of the stuff looks like it was just left. We brought back all of the stuff that we could carry. Deschaine got a nice AK-47, brought it in, and cleaned it up. He said that he is going to carry it for a while. It is a nice-looking weapon. Of course, we have seen them before, but this one is fairly new. So he is going to carry it for a while and see what he can shoot with it. Our patrol would have been a nice squad patrol. I was right behind second squad. By the time they moved out, first squad was coming around the corner and was headed back in. So I think that we covered the whole area. It was almost like having a first line of defense out there. By the time the first group was coming in, the last group was going out, so it was more than we really needed.

I got back in at 1430, and I just pulled off my boots and said, "What the hell. I'm going to lie here and relax a little bit." I just kind of laid around the area. It was really a nice spring day here.

It was a beautiful evening too. I had the second watch, and I really didn't have anything happening on the radio. The LPs were real quiet. Somebody else set them in; I didn't know where they were for sure.

We were told to get ready to go tomorrow morning. We are going to move on north through the valley. I had better sleep well tonight; it may be a while before I sleep in a good secure area.

April 10

I was up at 0600. We saddled up right away and moved down the hill and on up the valley. It took us most of the day just to move 3000 meters. The brush was really thick and we were moving real slow. We were in columns, and it was just one step at a time. We thought that we would set in at the old Lang Dah To Village; it's completely gone now. There is nothing left, but we thought it was a nice place to set in and we would have some water. The battalion wanted Bravo Company and Alpha Company in there, so they had us move on up.

A lieutenant from Alpha Company—I didn't see it, but I came by right after it happened—lost the pin out of a grenade and blew himself in two. It wounded two other guys; the other two guys weren't hurt too seriously. They were walking real close to him. One of them was a radio operator.

When we got set in, I went back and started talking to the guys in the platoon. I found out that a bunch of them had these little packets. We didn't know what they were at first. The guys had been picking them up; they were lying around all over the place. Then we got the word that they are actually little tiny explosive packages. A couple of guys were playing with them, and they went off. They are sort of like firecrackers. We didn't know what they were for, but they told us to leave them alone. I guess one guy from Bravo Company had a bunch of them in his pocket and blew a chunk out of his leg. I told all of the guys to leave the damn things alone and not to mess with them. Some guy from intelligence came by and told us what they were for. They drop this transmitter, which looks like a big tube. We saw one standing over in the woods. They are about 6 feet tall. They stick in the ground, and they drop all these little packages around. Then when the gooks walk through, they tramp on those little packets, and they explode. This tube picks up the sounds and transmits them back to the base. It tells them how many people are walking through the area. It is a pretty neat idea. The only thing is that these stupid kids won't leave them alone. We will be lucky if we don't get somebody hurt seriously with them. I was walking along watching for them and being careful, when I suddenly tramped on one. I could feel the vibration in my foot. It picked up my foot a little bit, but it really didn't hurt me.

We got everything set in. Everybody was lined up for the night, and all the patrols looked like they were ready to go. We were right beside what looked like a 1000-pound bomb crater. It was full of water, so a bunch of us peeled off our clothes and jumped in. It was nice; this was the first time I have really been in water for a long time other than to wash my face and hands. It was really nice. A couple of guys had bars of soap, so we got a nice bath. Deschaine and I were the first ones in. It was nice. Of course, after we did it, everybody else was in. The colonel called, and I guess he really got after the skipper pretty hard about it. But after we had been there for a while, it was about 1800, the colonel called down to the skipper and said go ahead and let us swim. So I went back in again. It was nice; the whole platoon in these big craters. It was bigger than any swimming pool I have ever been in. I don't know how deep it was out in the middle, but I couldn't touch the bottom. It was really nice to get in there and just swim around a little bit. It was hotter than hell, and this was really a nice way to cool off.

I caught Martin [Carlos G. 2363810] sleeping on watch. I don't know what the story was with him. I woke his ass up real quickly. Corbett only set out one man on watch. I don't know why he did that. I will have to talk to him about that tomorrow. Everything seems great; I'm going to sleep.

April 11

We moved out of our lovely beach house this morning. We moved out about 0630. We were moving up the hill. We moved about 300 meters real slow. We were really being careful. Since the Battalion Commanding Officer was running this operation, I suppose that they were going to make us move at a snail's pace. We got about 1000 meters from what we thought our objective was going to be. It started to pour down rain. I mean, it put it down so hard that for about an hour you couldn't even see. They told us to just set in and we would move on out after the rain stopped. So we set in on this little hill. It was tough; you had to chop a hole to make any kind of hooch to get your butt down at all. We made a hooch the best we could. I got the troops dug in and everybody was set up in our perimeter. We just laid around the rest of the day.

I don't understand why they were doing this. I mean here we were, 1000 meters from our objective. There were gooks all over the place. Even after the rain you could smell them. We knew the gooks were out there. You could tell that they were out there. But they had us set in here. It is an OK place. It is as good a place as any to set in. But we just wasted the rest of the day; we just sat here.

Husky took his squad out on an ambush tonight. They went out about 100 meters outside the perimeter and set in along the edge of the trail. I hope that everything goes OK with him. I made radio contact with them when I was on watch. They keyed the handset once when I asked if everything was OK, so I assume that it is.

Puyol is on the LP, and I hope that he stays awake. He is off to the right of them maybe fifty meters, so I hope that they don't shoot each other.

I just sat up with Gunny Ross and Staff Sergeant Myrick [George E. 1930707], listening to the radio. Since I am now platoon sergeant it is a tough situation. I am still a corporal and part of the platoon, and I would like to be friends with those guys. But some of the Marine Corps chain of command says that I am not supposed to be doing that. So it was nice to sit around and talk to these guys, although they are older than I am and pretty much lifers. They will probably be in a long time. But it was nice to sit around and talk to somebody and share some things. Even though I was the youngest and my goals are somewhat different from theirs, I really needed that. I needed to be able to sit down and talk to them for a while. I need to be friends with someone.

April 12

I guess they had a little trouble on Husky's ambush last night. Luster told Coleman to sit up and pay attention to what was going on. They had some kind of an argument. After they got back in, Coleman wanted to bring it up again and kind of got in Luster's face. But Luster was right. I knocked Coleman around a little bit and told him that I wasn't going to put up with that kind of shit. He has a job to do and responsibility falls on his shoulders to protect the rest of the men in the platoon, and he goes to sleep; that is not what we want.

I just hung around the area and did a little knife throwing. I never was any good at that, but Deschaine and I were throwing knives at this tree. We were just doing something to kill time. We were just sitting around bullshitting!

At 1145 we pulled out and moved on up the valley to Hill 758. Charlie Company took three KIAs and two WIAs. One KIA was from our own artillery.

My troops were on the LZ when the gooks decided to throw a couple mortars at us. We had three WIAs—two men from our weapons platoon, I don't know who they were, but they said there were two guys from our weapons platoon. I don't know who the other guy was, but they all three got hurt pretty bad. They medevaced them right out. They pulled us down off the hill, so I didn't really get to see who it was. The Corpsmen were taking care of them, and they pulled us back down the hill a little bit. They left the top of the hill just strictly for the LZ. We had to spread out and protect the LZ from down the hill.

Charlie Company had an FO with them who was calling in fire when a sniper got him. They said it took him right through the side of the head. We are out of an FO for our outfit for right now.

Thank God we will be getting out of this valley tomorrow. Maybe we can find some NVA. So far we haven't done much. We have taken a few WIAs and fired a few rounds, but I don't think that any of us have gotten off a clean shot. The gooks seem to be pulling back away from us. We find gear and weapons and all kind of things, but we are not able to find the gooks, so I think they realize that we are coming at them. We are pressuring them. They are moving back away from us.

A funny thing happened today. I almost had a CH-34 land right on my hooch. I was just lying there half asleep, and all of a sudden there was this chopper sitting right on top of me. I couldn't believe what I was seeing. I hadn't felt the wind off his blades or heard him, but he was right on top of me. I stood up on a pile of dirt and was trying to wave him on up the hill. I knew that he was there for a medevac. The LZ was on up the hill a little further. I kept waving and waving and waving. It was really hard to see the pilot from where I was, but we finally got him moved on up the hill to the LZ.

I'm going to try to get some sleep. Lt. Asmus said he will try to keep the choppers off me.

April 14

We didn't have our company minus. I don't know why; no one ever said, but we didn't go. We are getting ready to move back to Khe Sanh. The CO said that we are going back to Khe Sanh and flying out on another operation the next day. I don't know where we are going to go, but the Army is taking over Khe Sanh Combat Base. We are going to move back in and gather up what gear we have left and move out.

We didn't do much most of the day. We just laid around here, waiting for the word to move out. At 1330 we got the word we were staying another night. I had the troops redig their holes and set in their hooches a little better.

The troops are really feeling bad. I don't know what the problem is. Perhaps it is because we haven't had any contact or just the way things are going. I am feeling kind of blue myself. I don't know or I really can't put my finger on it, but everybody seems to be really down. Part of it is the guys we know got wounded and killed, and we really haven't been able to take a shot at anybody.

The chaplain came down to our area and said Mass about 1400. It's the first time I have gone to Mass out in the bush. It was really nice. It was short; it lasted about 15 minutes. It was kind of nice to go to Mass and just take 15 minutes and try to relax. One thing that the chaplain said was that we couldn't be too long or they'd bracket us in and drop one on us. We would get killed going to Mass, and we didn't want that to happen.

The company CO came by at 1630 and told us that we were going to move out as soon as it got dark. They didn't tell us exactly what time, but it would be O dark hundred. As usual, it didn't happen; maybe tomorrow.

April 15

We didn't pull out last night. They told us to sit tight. We are going to sit on this hill for a couple more days. They pulled the Marines off 881 and some of their gear. They said they are going to take the troops off 861 too. It looks like the Army is going to take over the hills as well.

I just laid around the area most of the day. I haven't been sleeping well at night at all, so I did get a little bit of sleep during the day (a couple of hours off and on). It is really depressing here. I don't know, we are really feeling tense. I don't think Marines are cut out to be in defensive positions. We have got to be on the offense. Sitting here on this hill is just not exactly what we like to do. We had a few incoming mortars up on the hill today. We didn't hear of any WIAs; everybody was able to stay out of the way.

The CO said we are going to move out at 0500. I hope that we get off this hill tomorrow. I don't want to stay here any longer. It won't be long before Charlie has us zeroed in, and he will be dropping artillery rounds and mortars in our lap.

Bravo went out to Hill 558 and said that they got a prisoner. I don't how they got him, if they found a wounded man or what. They brought somebody back, they said.

Deschaine, lieutenant, and I don't have watch anymore. I have to get some sleep.

April 16

We were up at 0400 and got ready to pull out. We got all the gear gathered up and ready to move. We pulled off the hill at 0700. We walked in columns down to the river. We were moving real slow. I know that there are gooks in the area; you can smell them. We stopped at the river for about an hour. Then we moved on back into Khe Sanh. We went into 1/9 area. It looked like we were going to stay there for a period of time, but then the word came to move on back over to Grey Alpha.

When we got to Grey Alpha, I couldn't believe it. Here we had worked so hard to get this place squared away and to keep the bunkers up and make it a decent living place. You don't really think of it as being home, but it is home. It is something that we were proud of. We worked hard to keep this place squared away. When the Army came, they just threw shit all over the place. There was garbage and trash all over the place. It was terrible. I mean, how did they live in this shit? You can't live in this kind of squalor. I was really disappointed, and I know that the troops were upset too. We gave all that we had, and this place was home for us. Now it looks more like a garbage dump. The Army had used one of our living bunkers for a shitter. We will never get that cleaned up. It was really unbelievable. I put the troops to work cleaning it up. They really didn't seem to mind. They were disappointed and disgusted at the way it looked, but they went right at it and got the place cleaned up.

I made a two-line roster even though we are supposed to pull out tomorrow. I want to be prepared. I don't want to take any chances. The way the situation has been going now, they tell us one thing and we end up doing something else.

I was really tired. I hit the rack at 1930 but was up at 2205. Coleman blew himself up. We went out with flashlights to see if we could find parts of him. You don't want to be out there too long with flashlights looking around, but we found his upper body. He had blown off both his legs, his lower half of his body, and one arm. We couldn't find all of him in the dark. We found one leg and part of his hip. We put what we found in a body bag and took it to graves registration.

We couldn't figure out what happened to Coleman. He was outside the bunker, one of the guys said, and he was by himself. I think that maybe he had a grenade in his pocket that went off. I didn't hear the explosion, but the guys came and woke me up. It was a mess. He had a flak jacket on, so it looked like he must have had the grenade inside the pocket of his flak jacket. We have got to find the rest of his body. We will try to do it in daylight. Nobody really wanted to go out there with a flashlight. It is too easy to get picked off, so we will get at it first thing in the morning and see if we can find what is left of him. Maybe we can find out what happened. It is really hard to say. We could find part of his flak jacket, but the other part of his flak jacket was missing. Maybe we can find out what caused it, maybe not.

One of the things that they say is that when you are a platoon sergeant, you take responsibility for all of your troops. Here is another one that I had to lose. I really feel bad about it. Of course, you can't live their life; I know that. But you try to do the best that you can. You try to direct them and show them what is right and how to be safe. I know that we all take chances. I did too when I was in his situation. It is just really sad to lose another trooper. I didn't know him real well, but he seemed like a good Marine to me.

April 17

I was up at 0400 trying to figure out what happened to Coleman. The only thing that we could figure out was that he was holding a claymore. The grenade went off, setting the claymore off. We hunted around and found his other leg blown down beside the bunker. We gathered it up; there were still parts of his body lying around. We tried to clean up what we could and took it up to graves registration. It looks like that is what happened. Whatever he had in his hand and was playing with just went off. It may have been some of those explosive pouches that we found when we were out in the field. Maybe he had some of those, and one of those set a grenade off. I supposed that we will never really know what happened.

We saddled up at 1100 and moved over to the runway. We were supposed to go out on a C-130, but it didn't show, so we just hung around and finally left on a CH-46.

The 46 came in and loaded us up and took us to our new home, a place called Wonder Beach. It is a real secure area. There doesn't seem to be any gooks in the area at all. It will be nice to relax. We set in at the left side of the base behind Bravo Company. I have 24 men from our platoon and myself. I'm not sure where Lt. Asmus and the rest of the troops are.

Top took all the platoon sergeants to a little party. I drank quite a few beers, and I'm really feeling pretty good right now. I got a little ribbing about being a corporal and being a platoon sergeant, but I think that most of the guys were just poking fun and joking around. They weren't seriously trying to hurt me, and I'm really proud of myself anyway. Here I am a corporal, but I'm doing the job of a platoon sergeant. I don't mind doing that.

I am pretty wasted, but I did find my way back. Asmus and 22 of the guys haven't shown up yet; I hope that they make it here tomorrow. There is nothing that I can do about it tonight, and I'm not going to worry about it. I need to go to sleep and sober up.

April 18

I was up at 0600, and I'm really feeling foul. I couldn't believe how bad I felt.

The part of the platoon that's here and I had four cases of beer today. The first couple went down hard.

I went with the platoon commanders to look at our lines. I checked it out and stayed. The platoon minus got over here at about 1400. We got the guys together and set up the areas. I got them set in and showed them where I wanted them to dig and so forth. We are getting our perimeter set up no mater what happens or how many guys we have.

I just fooled around until about 1700, then went to chow. It is nice to have hot chow again. I met some guy at chow I went through staging with. I couldn't remember his name, but we sat around and talked a little bit. Wonder Beach is his home base. Wonder Beach is a Cobra helicopter pad. Today was the first time I had ever seen a Cobra helicopter. I went over to the runway to check them out. It is a really sharp-looking chopper. The pilots sit one behind the other. One is a gunner and one actually flies the ship. It is really a sharp-looking machine.

I had a few more beers; I wasn't going to drink quite as many tonight as I did last night. It was nice to sit down, relax, and just really enjoy being alive.

I set the watches in. I had to send four people over to 2nd Platoon's sector. They needed some help over there because the rest of their platoon is not here either.

Washington and Martin can't be found. I don't know where they went. Hopefully they ran into some buddies. It's not all that important that they be with us right now, but we have got to get them rounded up. I will be glad when the lieutenant gets here with the rest of the platoon. He can handle all this shit, and I won't have to worry about it.

April 19

I was up at 0400. I had the last watch, but there is not much to do. You just sit and listen to the radio. Washington showed up late last night, and I put him right on watch. Wouldn't you know it, I caught him and Stewart [Billy, 2354494] sleeping.

I had the troops fill some sandbags. I figured that if we are going to be here, we might as well make it as safe as we can, so we filled some sandbags and dug some fighting holes. We don't really have a trench to work out of, but at least we have the fighting holes.

Gunny got a Mite someplace. I don't know where he got it—from the Army, I guess. Staff Sgt. Myrick and I rode around with him and checked out the base. We went down into the ocean. One thing about Wonder Beach that I didn't realize is that it is actually a beach. It is a real nice place.

Lieutenant Asmus and the rest of the troops showed up at about 1400. I was really glad to see him get here.

I took the platoon to chow and on the way back got into it with Langston (full name and service number not available). I don't know what his problem is. I think that he could really kick my ass if he tried. I don't want to get into a really physical confrontation with him. The squad leaders went to the lieutenant and told him that I had been riding them too hard, but like the lieutenant said, that is my job. If I wasn't riding them hard, this place would be awful slack. It did kind of piss me off, but not too much. I think that I can live with it. No beer tonight, just sleep.

April 20

I was up at 0700. I just had some chow and fooled around until 1000. They wanted us to take a patrol out, so I went out with a platoon-sized patrol. We just walked around the outside of the base and away from the ocean. We saw a few civilians; at least we thought that they were civilians. They could be VC; we don't know. We didn't have to shoot any of them anyway.

I went with Gunny Ross and Myers down to the beach. The 3rd Platoon was down there. They threw Myers and me in the water. I stayed for a few beers. It was nice. It is like being on vacation. I guess you could call this in-country R&R. Going from Khe Sanh to Wonder Beach is a big difference. It was nice to just sit there and soak up the sun a little bit and lie around the water and drink a few beers. It kind of reminded me of being back near Charleston or Myrtle Beach when I was down there a few years ago. I had a platoon-sized ambush at 2100. I really wasn't too excited about that because I think that taking a whole platoon out on an ambush is a joke. There are too many people, and you really can't set it up very well. Lieutenant handled all of the setting in and everything. I probably would have done it a little bit different, but it worked. We didn't set the ambush off, but everything was OK. We got back in at 0530, and everybody was alive and well. I don't think there is a gook within 100 miles of here.

April 21

This was Sunday. I can't remember when I knew what day of the week it was. I went to chow at 0700. It is really nice to get some hot chow. I really enjoyed it. I came back, went to sleep, and slept until 0945. I went to church. It seemed funny to go to Mass without sweating the incoming. We had Mass outside. It really wasn't a church, but it was nice not to worry about somebody shooting you. Mass was a little longer today than the last one I went to, and I didn't have to worry about somebody killing me.

I had to go to a platoon commanders' meeting for Lt. Asmus. I don't know exactly where he went, but he said he had to go somewhere else. So I went to the meeting. In the meeting the only thing we talked about was a new place battalion wants to set us in, a new area where we are going to take over the lines. I knew then why the Lt. sent me to the meeting; it was a bunch of bullshit.

I went down to the beach. I got down there at about 1200; the rest of the guys were already down there. I had a few beers and did some swimming. It wasn't real hot today. The sun wasn't out bright, so it was nice. You know, it is really relaxing. I think that the powers that be figured this out. This is a place for Delta Company to be. I think that they made the right choice this time. It is a nice place to relax.

Lieutenant put Markum as first squad leader. McCulley, who was the squad leader, went back to his fire team. McCulley didn't seem too disappointed. McCulley didn't really want to do it, and I'm not sure that he was very good at it anyway. He is a good kid, but he just doesn't have what it takes to kick ass when it has to be done to carry out the order.

We had a formation for promotion. It is something that we haven't had the chance to do for a while. The guys knew that they had been promoted. Markum, Green, Mitchell [Homer, 240873I], and Verschage all got promoted. It was pretty nice. We haven't had a formation like this for a long time, where the guys all got together and were happy for each other, so it really turned out to be a pretty good day.

April 23

I was up at 0600 and had a patrol at 0700. We went out about 1600 meters and set up. We just ran a few patrols from there. We were just out to see what we could find. There is not too much going on. It is really strange, though. The terrain here is so much flatter that it was at Khe Sanh. There are a lot of rice paddies and things. It is easier to move around. We came back in and worked on our new holes for the rest of the day.

I am not working too hard; I'm just working at about half speed. I made a promise to myself last night that I would be a little easier on the troops. That is what I am going to try and do starting today. I am going to talk to them in a way that will show them a little more respect. Maybe that will make them do the job better, and I will have less trouble with them. I'm not going to let up too much, just stop being such a hard ass.

I went out on night patrol at about 2000. We went out about 50 meters and everybody started firing flares. We didn't want to be walking along making such an easy target, so we sat there for about two and a half hours. It was really strange, we just sat there. I was lying on the ground and went sound asleep along with everybody around me. The rest of the patrol moved out and didn't even say a word to us. They hadn't gone very far when one of the guys woke up and got the rest of us up. We jumped up and caught up to them without any problem. It was a little scary for a minute or two, though. What if we caught up to them, they thought we were gooks and started shooting at us? We knew where they were going, so it wasn't hard to catch up. We got back in at 0215, and I am going to hit the sack now.

Tomorrow we are going to have a little beach party, I think, so we will see what happens. I'm anxious to see how the troops treat me when we are on more of an equal ground. I felt I was different today.

April 24

I got up at about 0800 and went to chow. We were all set to head down to the beach when gunny came by and told us that the guns were going to do it today. We were not going to do it. So we just started filling sandbags and got our hooches ready to go. Fox and I filled about 200 sandbags. One of the things that I am trying to do now is make things a little more relaxed for the troops, so we set up a little challenge. We filled 200 sandbags. It worked pretty well.

Lieutenant and Deschaine were off someplace. I don't know where they went, but Deschaine came back about 1700. He went to work on the hooch. It was really cool because we could just drink a few beers and fill a few sandbags. Besides, it is free beer, which makes it even nicer. Deschaine got pretty smashed and was laughing and joking and carrying on. It was a pretty laid-back day.

Tomorrow is our beach party. We worked hard on these hooches, got them built up a little bit, and our fighting holes are ready to go. If we don't go to the beach tomorrow, I'll be as pissed off as the troops.

April 25

We worked pretty hard early on the bunkers and thought we were going to get our beach party. But it turned out that the powers that be had other things for us to do. They took us over to Bravo lines at about 1100. We worked with them for a while; we helped them set in some sandbags and do some things. We came back to our area at 1620. We just fooled around until 2130.

At 2130 we got the word that we had to saddle up the whole platoon and move out. A chopper had gotten shot down, and they wanted us to go see what we could find out about it. It was really strange because nobody was around. Part of the platoon was in the showers and the rest just fooling around in different areas. The lieutenant wasn't even there, so I got the troops rounded up the best that I could. It took us about an hour to get to the LZ. They flew us out on 46s. In about five minutes we were there. We set up our perimeter around what was left of a Huey helicopter. It was still burning. We couldn't tell what brought it down, but we could see some bodies in there. Although it was starting to get dark by the time we got there, we could see the bodies. The bodies were all burned. There was definitely nobody alive, so we really didn't have to worry about it too much. 3rd Platoon and weapons came out along with the skipper. He told us that we were just going to set in for the night.

We set up our perimeter and put out some LPs. We gave the LPs the word: if you see anything, shoot and di-di the hell back inside, and we will deal with the situation from there. At about 2300, Grothkof and Martin were out on LP, and they saw some people moving around, took a few shots, and came back in. We fired some flares and looked around and couldn't see anything. After everything settled down, I sent them back out. As of now they are still out there.

The helicopter is a real mess. This is the first time I have ever seen anything like this up close. Over at Khe Sanh I saw a lot of planes blown up and helicopters crashed, but I never really had to go out and do something with it. I could tell there was a black guy. You could tell by the type of hair that he had. You couldn't see his face. It was burned off. All you could see was the top of the head. It was still burning, so I poured some water on it. I didn't want to pour too much on it, and a couple guys pissed on it because you don't want to waste your water when you don't know how long you are going to be out here. We tried to get the fire out and get his body to stop burning. The piss seemed to do OK. It seems kind of sick to do something like that, but water is very important to us. We were not about to waste the water we had for drinking.

We don't have much of an area to protect ourselves in, but it will have to do for tonight. I don't think I'll sleep too well. When we get up in the morning, in the daylight we will see what we can do to try and salvage these bodies.

April 26

I was up at first light. We did the best we could to try and get the bodies out of the chopper. There were about six bodies in it, I would guess. They were so messed up, you couldn't tell one body from another. We were just pulling parts out. They were all burned beyond recognition. It was really strange. One guy's leg looked like something my mom used to cook. I don't know what it was called, but she had this piece of meat and it had something like a piece of rope or string around it. This guy's leg looked like that. As his flesh cooked, it swelled and the trouser leg burned away except where the seam was sown together. It just made a tight grip around the flesh of his leg. It reminded me so much of that meat that Mom used to cook on Sundays when I was growing up. I know it's strange to think that, but that's what it reminded me of.

We tried to put what we thought were the same parts of the bodies into the same bags. We wanted to keep the parts of each body together. We did find some dog tags and got those back in with the bodies. The one black body we found wasn't in too bad of shape. His head and face were all burned up, but hopefully his teeth will be in his mouth and they will be able to identify him. We didn't find his dog tags on him so I don't know if they will be able to identify him or not. Surely with the teeth they will be able to. There wasn't much left of the other bodies; they were really burned up. We tried to put them in the body bags as best we could and get them back to the base. I hope they can be identified so their families will have something to bury. We blew up the rockets and destroyed whatever else was left of the chopper and started back to the base.

The hump back in wasn't too bad. We stopped at about 1400 in a real nice grassy area. It was almost like a golf course. My feet were hurting like everyone else's, so we pulled our boots off. I was walking in the nice grass and as I stepped forward, the ground gave away and I was above a punji pit. Thank God I was walking really slowly. As I went down, my foot touched the tip of a stick. I was able to fall to the side and not directly down into the pit. I did get a small cut on my foot. I put on some stuff I had in my first aid kit, so I hope it will be OK. We got back in about 1530.

After we had chow and cleaned up a little bit, Heath came over and we hated the Corps together. I think we both are pretty fed up with the war. Before we left Khe Sanh I was thinking about shipping over and making a life in the Corps, but not now. If I get out of Nam I am getting out. My foot hurts and I'm tired.

April 27

I didn't get up in time for chow this morning. I just didn't feel like it. I had a Corpsman put some stuff on my foot, and it feels better tonight.

I just hung around the area and worked on our hooches. I must have filled about 100 sandbags today. I had a patrol at 2100. We took the platoon out and left Markum's squad out there for an ambush. We left the wire at 2100 with 45 men. We had a really lousy patrol. I don't know who was in charge of setting this thing up, but the area we had to cover was too small for a whole platoon. The whole platoon was never outside the wire at one time. When the front of the platoon was starting back in, the rear group was just going out. We left Markum's squad along the road and brought everyone back in. I hope he has a safe ambush tonight. That's like saying I hope he kills a lot of people and is safe doing it.

The scariest part was that the patrol was set up so we went out the east side of the base, crossed to the south, and back in on the west side of the base. When we came back up along the road and were coming back into the base, we had to cross right in front of H&S Company about 100 meters out. I was a little bit worried about them taking a few shots at us not knowing who we were. We did get back in OK and didn't have any contact.

I don't have any watches tonight, so I will get a good night's sleep.

April 28

Today is Sunday. This is first Sunday since I have been in Vietnam that it felt like a real Sunday. I enjoyed last Sunday, but today was better, I didn't get up until 1000 and went to Mass.

Deschaine went over to work for the chaplain, but he didn't have any work for him, so he came back and we just sat around all day and shot the bull.

The only bad thing that happened today was when Markum's squad came back in, someone from H&S Company fired on them. No one got hit, and they made it back in OK. I would like to find the bastard that shot on them. We went over to the lines but nobody would say who had been firing at us. I think we scared the hell out of a few guys. We are here from Khe Sanh, and I think most of the guys stationed here full time think we are crazy.

It was a nice, relaxing but strange Sunday. As long as I have been in Nam I couldn't tell one day from the next. You never knew what day it was and never really cared anyway. It was a nice sunny day. It kind of reminded me of a spring day back in West Virginia. On Sundays at my house you never worked, never had to do anything except take care of the animals. We did kill a chicken every Sunday and clean it and Mom would fry it up for dinner. We never did any real work, and that was how it was around here today. We all just sort of relaxed and took it easy. I think being here at Wonder Beach, even though we are running a few patrols and doing something out in the bush, is a lot more relaxed than at Khe Sanh. We don't feel the pressure that we were under at Khe Sanh. So it really turned out to be a great day. I guess God was on our side and gave us a nice Sunday. I'm not sure God picks sides in war, but he did give us a nice day.

I think I will sleep good tonight.

April 29

I slept really well. I really didn't want to get up until I really had to, but Corbett and Huskey kept fooling with me. They wanted me to take a formation to chow. This is like being back at Camp Lejeune, we move in formation.

I worked on my hooch a little bit today. I finished the walls and put up a screen door. I found the door over in the Army barracks area. They had a hooch with this screen door on it that was about to fall off. Nobody was around so I helped the door fall off. I brought it back to my hooch and put it up. It didn't have any hinges on it, so I used rope. It looks kind of cool and lets the air blow right through a little bit. It might even keep a few of the bugs out.

I have a patrol tomorrow. We are going to sweep down through this ville off to our southeast. We have about 40 tanks and a bunch of armored personnel carriers going with us. This ought to be a real joke. I don't know how well I can communicate with the tank commanders or how well anybody can. It's like they do things their own way and to hell with everybody else. So hopefully it won't be too big of a cluster fuck and we will get through it without any trouble. I hope our own guys don't shoot us.

We will be pulling out early, so I hope I can get some sleep tonight. It sure is quieter than it was at Khe Sanh.

April 30

I was up at 0330 and got the troops ready to go. We moved down to the gate at 0430. Eckhart [Gerald, 2218659] didn't get his guns out with us until we were outside the wire. It really pissed me off because we were ready to move out but we had to wait for him.

We had just gotten outside the wire when the CO stopped us, and we just sat there for several minutes. The word came down for us to move back inside the wire. We then fooled around for another hour because the tanks hadn't gotten into position. They said that two companies of gooks had hit the tank base.

We moved out at 0930. We went out about 2000 meters and were told to stop. They moved us up to be a blocking force for Alpha Company. We moved up through Alpha and they moved us again. We were then told to go after the NVA that had hit the tanks, so we started to move off in that direction.

We humped out about 8000 meters. About that time an APC came up and loaded us up, so we rode for probably another 3000 meters. They let us off at a railroad bridge and we set up with some ARVN. The ARVN moved over toward the ville and we stayed at the bridge. The ville was right across the river but it look more like a creek to me. We sat there doing nothing until 1530, then moved back to Alpha area.

It was really a screwed-up mess, but I knew it would be. Just give me my platoon and we will kick some gook ass. When you put all these other assholes together it's fucked up. Nobody seemed to know what anybody else was doing. I understand we don't know the area, but we have radios, so we should be able to get shit done. Anytime we get above a company-sized patrol it seems like everything gets screwed up.

We sat in with Alpha for about an hour, then we were told to move out about 1000 meters into the bush and set in for the night. It was about 1630 when we got into position.

It looked pretty quiet, and I guess after being in Khe Sanh, every place looks pretty quiet. We just set in as best we could.

Bravo is across the river from us. We just heard them take 60 mm fire. We didn't hear what happened; maybe we will hear tomorrow.

When we came through the ville today I did see some women. I don't know if they were VC or civilians but they were good-looking. This was the first time I had seen any good-looking women since I left Hong Kong. I didn't see any of my guys fooling with them, and I hope they don't, but we will see what happens tomorrow.

I'm going to try to get some sleep, and I hope I can make it through the night without getting killed.

May 1

I was up at 0530. My foot is really hurting where I cut it yesterday. I don't know what I am going to do. The Lt. told me to go see the Corpsman, but I don't want to do that and leave the troops but I may have to.

We just sat around until 1400. Then we moved across a couple dry rice paddies. It was really strange walking across these rice paddies. It just seems like walking across a dry oats field. The paddies are dry now and it is easy to get through them.

The orders were to go into and sweep through this ville. It was real tense. We took some small-arms fire, and we fired a few rounds back into the ville. But we didn't find anybody. We got on APCs and tanks and moved on down across the river about 200 meters and set in. Nobody seems to know what the hell is going on. They loaded the 3rd Platoon on a recoilless rifle and moved them on down a little further toward the woods. The skipper said that he couldn't figure out where we are. The maps that he has don't seem to coordinate with the fields that we are in. We were supposed to be a blocking force for a battalion of ARVN, but we are not sure that is what we are supposed to be doing now. It seems like everything changes all of the time. Someone decided to move 3rd Platoon back up to the area where we left this morning. Then they decided to move all of us back to the road. They moved us back up to the road, and we set in there for a while. Then they decided we were supposed to go down to Alpha Company area, but they changed their minds again. They brought us all back in to Wonder Beach. What a mess of a day. I knew it would be. I knew it yesterday when they talked about all of the troops that were going to be involved. They just never seem to be able to coordinate this size of a patrol. It was just a mess of a day.

Intelligence told us that we are supposed to get some rockets fired in on us tonight. I don't know where they get that information, but we are ready to go. The CO said that there are two battalions of NVA digging in about 300 meters outside of our AO. They are supposed to be in 1st Air Cav's area, so I hope that they do something about them. They can fire rockets into our laps without any problems from that distance.

It is going to be a rough night tonight. It has been a terrible day. One of the most miserable days I have had since I have been in Vietnam. I hope that I can sleep a little bit tonight.

May 2

The day started off early. We were up at 0200 and moved the troops down to Charlie lines. Charlie Company is moving out into the Auchsha Valley. It seems that the gooks have pulled away from Khe Sanh somewhat, but they have moved back up into the valley.

Bravo got hit with RPGs, mortars, and small-arms fire last night, not 60s. So we know that the gooks are out there.

At 0700 I had to go to the battalion aid station. I just couldn't walk on my foot anymore. A Corpman named DeMag looked at my foot. Cut a little of the swelling away and put some stuff on it. He said that it would be OK. It is going to be sore for a few days. He told me the best that I could is to stay off it.

I went back down the lines and just sat there by myself. The platoon had gone out on a work detail, so I was just there by myself. I couldn't wait for them to get back, though. My job is to be with my platoon, and I didn't like staying there by myself. I tried to read a book, but I couldn't concentrate. All that I could think about was what they were doing. I was really glad when they got back.

I took the Mite and was riding around, and when I went back past the company office, the top stopped me and told me to find Hensen [Clark, L. 2063752]. He said that he had gotten our warrants and he wanted us to come up to the company office. I went out and got Hensen. The captain came out and gave the warrants to us. It was really cool. Myers held a Coleman lantern while the skipper read the warrants. It was really a neat deal. I am now an E-5 sergeant. I was glad to get it. Of course, Heath already got his a while back, so he got appointed to be the first to pin our stripes on. The gunny and the top pinned them on too. Pinning on your stripes is having anybody senior to you hit you on the arm where the stripes will go when sewed onto your shirt. Lt. Asmus acted like he was going to pin them on, but he didn't. I wouldn't have cared if he had hit me; he's more of a friend than a platoon commander. He said someone might not like an officer pinning stripes on a sergeant. It makes me feel a lot better being a sergeant, as a platoon sergeant. At least I am moving up the ranks now.

We had to go out on another night patrol tonight. I pulled out with the platoon at 2000 hrs. It's taken about seven hours just to go out around the land sides of the base. We moved real slow but made it back in one piece.

I feel better tonight than I ever have since I've been in Nam. I'm proud of myself. It's funny how your emotions change from one day to the next. Last night I felt as bad as I ever have since I've been in here. Tonight I feel great, I feel like somebody important and well liked. I really hate to go to sleep tonight.

May 3

I got up at about 0830 and went to chow. I got back and just fooled around Charlie lines, waiting for them to come in. They got back in while we were at noon chow.

We moved back up to our area, and they told us to be ready to move out on 15 minutes notice. We got the troops ready. We got all of our gear ready to go. If and when they call us, we should be able to be on choppers in 15 minutes.

Heath and I went to the staff and officer's club and had quite a few beers. We could hardly find our way back. We had a great time, I think.

I got some real sad news today. It really upset me. Captain Champion told me that Major Loughran [Joseph M. [No service number available] had been killed today. Major Loughran was my CO when I was aboard the *USS Canopus* (AS-34). I was a security guard. I got to know him really well; I stood honor guard at his wedding. I really felt worse about him being killed than anyone else that I've known who has been blown away. He was really a great guy. He took time to listen to us. I was a lance corporal and corporal when I was serving with him, and he was a super guy. He really treated me well. He and Lt. Asmus are the best damn officers in the Marine Corps. The captain said that Major Loughran was out on patrol with his battalion and tramped on a mine and he bled to death before the chopper could get him out. I really feel sorry for his family. I know that he just had a baby. I hope that his wife, Julie, and baby make out OK. I didn't know Julie real well, but she seemed nice. Julie, my prayers are with you tonight.

I will sleep some tonight, I hope. Tonight as I lay here I won't be feeling sorry for myself; I will be praying for a lost friend and a great Marine.

May 4

I woke up at about 0700. I am hurting. I think that this is the worst hangover that I have ever had. Heath is in no better shape. I just fooled around the area until noon. I couldn't really do anything. I couldn't even think. I couldn't talk until 1545. They told us to saddle up and to move out. Word came down from the company commander, and all of the lieutenants are down at the beach. The skipper was really pissed. We loaded on trucks, and we rode inland for about two hours. We stopped at a helicopter pad named LZ Sharon south of Da Nang. They said it was about eight clicks south. We go hot chow and all of the cold beer that we could drink. Heath and I had one apiece. We decided to swear off of the stuff for a while. We set in for the night inside their perimeter. We are supposed to move out about 600 meters to Hill 34 to set up as soon as the rest of the battalion gets up here, if they come. It's really kind of nice, we are sleeping under the stars tonight, and it is a beautiful night, but the damn mosquitoes are just eating us up.

May 5

Today was Lt. Asmus's and my birthday. The gooks held reveille on us at just about daylight. We had ten rounds of rockets come firing in. We are out on the perimeter, and they hit in through the middle of the base somewhere.

None of them landed very close to us. It did scare the hell out of me, though.

What a wonderful way to start my birthday. I am 22, and Lieutenant Asmus is 25 today. I got a pair of sunglasses from Hall with one lens missing, and box of cookies from Markum. The Lt. got a bush hat from someone. They were very special presents. No one here has anything of great value to give. The glasses, even with one lens missing, meant a lot to Hall and they mean a lot to me.

The guys broke into a conx box early this evening and brought back eight cases of beer. Someone found a little ice, enough to cool a six-pack. We had a cold beer and several warm ones.

We were told to move out on the lines, so we moved out to where we were going to set in. No bunkers, the place was really bad, but we will get it squared away. I don't know how long we will be here, but we are going to start digging in and getting the place squared away. At least we have hot chow. That's the only thing that I can say for this place. It's nice to get hot chow as often as you can.

I have been drinking beer all day. I was going to go out with Heath and Henson [Clark L., 2063752], but they both had to babysit. I tried to get the lieutenant to go out so that I could go out tomorrow night. We have to take turns now. The CO told us that there was no way both platoon sergeant and platoon commander could be away from the platoons at the same time, so we have to take turns babysitting. I would like to get it set up so that Heath and I could have the same nights off, but I don't think that it is going to happen because all of the lieutenants can't have the same night off.

I spent my 21st birthday in Vietnam. It wasn't too bad, though. I didn't get shot today, so that is something nice. We're sitting on the side of this hill and it's so steep we had to dig a place to put our ass so we didn't slide down the hill. I'm just sitting here drinking beer. I made a little bet with the guys sitting here with me: the first guy to pass out will get pissed on by the others. So I am just going to keep drinking beer until I can't drink beer anymore. Then I am going to pass out. If they piss on me, they piss on me.

May 6

I stayed up drinking as long as I could. It was 0200 when we got some rockets fired in on us, and it must have been shortly after that, I passed out. I guess nobody pissed on me. I didn't smell like piss when I woke up.

I didn't get up for chow this morning. I just laid there and let the sun shine on me. I couldn't move anyway. I don't know how many beers I drank to celebrate my birthday, but it was enough.

We had some recoilless rifles being fired at us, so the gooks have gotten in close.

We had a memorial service at 1630. That is the first time that we have done anything like that. It was on the battalion level, and it was for everybody who had been killed in the battalion. It was raining like hell, but we all stood out there. Nobody complained.

At 1735 we got the word to move out. We got on the 6-bys and moved into Quang Tri. We rode around looking for 1/26 rear for damn near an hour. It is strange; nobody seems to know where anything is here. We got here at about 2100. Puyol left some of my gear on the truck, so I had to go find the damn truck and get it back.

We are going to sleep inside the base tonight. We don't have any watches or any LPs to set out, so we will just sleep here in hoochs tonight. It will be kind of nice to be inside.

May 7

I was up at 0600 and loaded on a truck again. They told us that we were moving toward Dong Ha. They said that there were a lot of gooks around, but we are driving up these roads. I hope that somebody is doing a little minesweeping out in front of us. We got into Dong Ha and just sat around. It is a nice big base. It is almost as big as the one at Da Nang. At least it looks that way. They even had an E-5 mess. That was kind of cool, so Heath and I went to the mess hall together and just fooled around most of the afternoon.

At 1600 they loaded us on tanks and ferried us across the river. We moved north for a couple hours. They told us to set in for the night. There are supposed to be from five to eight regiments of gooks around the area. So, the NVA know where we are, and we don't know where they are.

The maps that they gave us show the DMZ, so I assume that we are someplace up around the DMZ, maybe across it. I don't know exactly where we are. The maps that we have don't seem to show. The terrain doesn't seem to match them yet. I think that we are in the north. The word is that we are going to be sweeping south just to the west of Dong Ha. We will know where we are when we get there. I don't think that I will sleep too well tonight.

May 8

I was up at 0400 and moving out with the tanks. I'm in charge of coordinating the tanks with our company. The tanks couldn't seem to keep up. They were off to our left flank and were moving with us, but it was hard to see them in the dark. I tried to keep up with them through radio contact, but they just weren't able to stay with us. It seemed like they couldn't see in the dark at all. Of course, none of them have any headlights, but there is nothing to worry about running over. So we did the best that we could.

I was with 3rd Platoon. During the time that I was trying to make radio contact with the tanks, I got separated from them. I had to haul ass to keep up. I don't like being out here by myself; that is for sure. The 1st Platoon did hold up until the rest of us caught up.

We moved through our first objective. We took about ten rounds of our own artillery. These gunners just can't seem to understand what is going on. Of course, our maps don't exactly tell where we are, so we don't know where we are. I am sure that it was our own artillery that hit us. Shirah [Raymond E., 2308370] got hit in the leg; Benten the Corpsman just went crazy. I think that it's from the pressure of being here and trying to help people and taking care of them. We had to medevac him too.

The 2nd Platoon took one KIA. It was like only 0815 in the morning. All of that had happened before 0900. It was really a bad situation. We were deep in the shit.

We finally moved out slowly and moved to our second objective without any contact. We moved on across to our last objective at 1420 and set in for the night.

Chambers [James L., 2369298] was the guy that got killed from 2nd Platoon, and we had services for him and the guys that got wounded. We just did it among ourselves, without the chaplain or anybody. We did that at 1930.

There are a whole lot of friendlies around the area. I mean it is really crowded with a whole bunch of people, tanks, and our whole battalion moving around, so we will probably get hit tonight by our own people. I won't sleep at all.

May 9

I was up at 0500. We didn't much feel like moving out, but we had to. There are so many friendlies, and we know that the gooks are around here someplace. We moved out about 1200 meters and set in for about 4 hours.

The strangest thing happened; we started to move out, and I heard gook voices off to our right flank. The squad I was with was on the right flank of the whole operation. The guys around me heard them too. It wasn't like we would make it up, but I don't think everyone believed us. The wind was blowing from the right, so we thought that maybe the wind had carried the voices toward us. I called the CO and told him that we heard voices off to our right flank, so he stopped the whole battalion. We were kind of in a sloping area with low hills, and the brush wasn't real thick. It was about waist deep. When I told the CO, he said, "OK, take a squad and fire sweep the area." We were just below the ridge of the hill, so we worked our way up, fired a few rounds, and moved across the top of the hill. We didn't find anything. We came back down, and Lieutenant Asmus called the skipper and told him. He relayed it on to the battalion commander. The battalion commander was really pissed. He was expecting some kills when we held up his whole battalion. It was not the thing to do. I understand that; we have a whole bunch of guys sitting here waiting for us. But I know that I heard voices; I could hear them just as plain as anything. The guys around me could hear them too.

We started moving out, moving forward again. We were moving in columns. We got down near this little opening where there wasn't any brush. There must have been a stream there at one time. We were moving down this little hill toward the open area. All of a sudden, Mitchell yelled and we saw five gooks moving out in front of us. We all knew that it was probably an ambush. I told the lieutenant. I said, "I am going to move up on the right flank. We have to be careful going down across there." We started down across the opening, on line about five meters apart. Just as we got out into the open area, all hell broke loose. Someone yelled that the lieutenant got hit. I was on the right flank and started running down through the open area to where the lieutenant was. As I was running down there, I could see Fox, the platoon radio man. He was being hit by the rifle fire. He was trying to fall forward, but he was really not falling because the bullets were hitting him and holding him up. I just tackled him like I was playing football and drove him over sideways. When I got down to where the lieutenant was, I could see that he had been shot. He was OK; it wasn't a really bad injury. But he had been shot. Another one of my guys was lying on his back doing a back bridge. When I rolled him over to me I saw the side of his head was gone and I couldn't tell who he was; I just held him in my arms until he stopped shaking and was dead. I laid my head down on his chest and said to myself, "I quit, I can't do this anymore." In the same two seconds I knew I had to pull myself together. I knew the responsibility for the platoon was mine. I was really scared. I thought of Charlie Morris, my high school English teacher and play director. He once told me, "When you are really frightened, take a deep breath and go to it." So that's what I did. I got the radio from Fox and tried to call in support. The only thing that I could think to do was to get the tanks to come in. There wasn't a whole lot of brush. The brush was probably 8 to 10 feet high right in front of us, but it wasn't really thick. I knew that the gooks were right in front of us. As I was talking on the radio, I had my 45 in my right hand and the radio handset in my left hand, and I was lying down pretty flat, as flat as I could get. All of a sudden, as I raised up, trying to see the tanks, a gook raised up maybe 6 feet away from me. He had an AK-47 in his hands. It was really strange; we made eye contact. I had never been that close to one. It scared me, and I am sure that he was scared too. But I was lucky; I had the 45. I turned and fired off two rounds. One hit him right through the chin and came out through the back of his head. The other shot went right through his chest. At about that time, one of the gooks threw a hand grenade, and as I was falling forward I heard it go off behind me. I felt the concussion in my boots and right in the base of my butt. I reached back. There was a hole in my trousers, but there wasn't any blood or anything, so I figured that it must have been just a stone.

I made contact with the tanks and the tank commander came on. I told him that the only thing that I could think to do was to have the tanks just drive across in front of us. (The tanks were maybe 500 meters away from us.) We would just let them drive across in front of us here and smash this brush down because the gooks were in trenches right in front of us. We couldn't move at all.

Part of the platoon was still back on the other side of the opening, and I got hold of Stripling and told him to bring that machine gun up. Just as he started across the opening, I could see him getting hit. Every time someone tried to move across from the other side up to where we were, they were getting hit, so I know that we couldn't do that.

I told the tank commander, "Just send those damn tanks over here and let them drive across in front of us. What do the gooks have that they are going to stop a tank with?" I didn't think that they had anything. I heard the tanks moving out, and the tank commander came up on our frequency. I told him I was going to throw a smoke grenade to mark our position. The only smoke that I had was a red one. I knew that red usually marked the spot to fire at, but that was the only color I had. I told him I would throw it, and for him to start firing their 50s, but not to fire to the right of that smoke. Just drive the tanks right up across this brush like a bulldozer. Just drive right across and fire your 50s to keep the gooks down. It should be OK. I threw the smoke grenade. All of a sudden, somebody else from the tanks comes on the radio and says I will hit them with my 90, I will hit the smoke with my 90. I thought, "Man, the smoke is going off right in my face; if he fires his 90, I am dead meat." So I am yelling, "NO! NO! Don't fire the 90! Don't fire to the right; our platoon is pinned down here! Don't fire to the right of the smoke!" He didn't fire, thank God. So I heard the tanks moving out; I could see them coming. They disappeared down in a little valley away from me, but I could hear them coming up toward me. All of a sudden I heard what sounded like an RPG and an explosion, and the tanks stop. I tried to call the tank commander and tried to get him to open the radio. He wouldn't come up; no one from the tanks would talk to us, and we were still pinned down.

Finally Charlie Company came up behind us, and they were firing some support. We were firing into this tree line. You couldn't see anything. We just fired blind. Charlie moved across to the edge of the tree line.

The top came down and was lying right beside me. He was trying to help me assess the situation. There wasn't anything he or anyone could do, but it did make me feel better. About that time, some young private came up where we were and got down. He was really scared; you could see he was shaking and trembling. We were all pretty scared. There were like five of us lying in this one little area. The squad leader said, "Come on; we are going to assault through this brush. Get up, we are going to go through this brush." The kid said, "I can't, I can't, I can't get up!" The squad leader said, "Come on, damn it, follow me." He jumped up and took about two steps, and this poor young private must have had his rifle on automatic. He just squeezed the trigger and cut his squad leader's legs right off. I crawled up where I could get him and pulled him back. We put tourniquets on his legs; he was going into shock. The kid that had shot him just laid down on top of him. He was screaming and crying. It was just a terrible situation.

Finally the rest of Charlie Company moved through, but it looked like the gooks had pulled back. I don't know how the rest of the battalion didn't see them, but when Charlie Co. went through they found only dead gooks.

I wasn't going through; I took what was left of my platoon and got our bodies and pulled back into a secure area where we could set up an LZ to get the wounded out. It was about 1630 then when we pulled back. We gathered up the wounded and got everybody as far back as would could get. We set a little perimeter around so that we could start getting people medevaced.

After I got the wounded out I went back up where I had killed the gook. I wanted to see him, I guess. I had hit him just as I thought, once in the head and once in the chest. I went through his pockets and found his wallet. When I opened it I found a picture of a woman and two kids. I suppose it was his family. I had killed the kids' dad and this woman's husband, and I'm glad I did it...right now, anyway.

During the course of the whole thing, the captain had gotten killed. He had come up beside Corbett, and Corbett kept telling him to stay down. "You're not John Wayne," I thought. He wouldn't listen. He stood up, and I know he was trying to encourage us and be a good leader. The gooks couldn't have been more than 10 meters away, and that 50 caliber just blasted his ass. I felt sorry for him, but I remember thinking, "How stupid. Who in the hell do you think you are?" Just because you are a captain doesn't mean that you are bulletproof, and he wasn't.

The gooks had us pinned down for about an hour and a half. And if the damn tanks would have done what I asked them to do, I think that we would have been a lot better off. We wouldn't have had as many people killed. But I found out later when I called the battalion commander and asked him what the hell happened to the tanks. I was pissed, and I called him up on the radio. I went up to see him, and he said that one of the guys had opened the front of the tank and was firing a Thompson out the hatch. He was just kind of spraying the area with a Thompson. The gooks fired an RPG and it hit the guy and blew him right back into the tank. The lieutenant that was the tank commander just shut the tanks down, sealed them up, and sat there. He is lucky that the whole damn mess wasn't blown away. They are going to write him up. I guess that he is going to be relieved of duty.

Fox, Hall, and Markum got hit pretty bad. They were still alive when we medevaced them out. Mitchell and Stewart are dead. We kept them here with us. All together we had 11 KIA's in our platoon; I don't know how many WIAs.

We finally got set in about 1800.

The saddest part of the day was when the chaplain came over from battalion, along with this doctor and a Corpsman. They were going through the body bags, making sure everyone that is there is dead. The priest gave them last rites. It was sad. Corbett and I sat there with our feet in the hole we had dug and cried like babies. We could get just our feet down in the hole. If the gooks hit us right now, they will wipe us out. We both just sat there and cried and cried. It is the saddest day of my life. We have all wanted to get into the shit like this for a long time, but I had no idea what it was really like. I can't believe that it was so bad. I suppose it was my fault that some of the guys were killed, but I did my best. I don't know if Stripling is dead or not, but we medevaced him out. I can still see him getting hit.

We are not going to do much tonight. We are just going to try and get some sleep. I do know that if the gooks hit us tonight, we are dead.

May 10

I was up at first light. The LP that we set out last night got hit with some shrapnel, but I think that it was from a grenade that he threw himself. So we had to medevac him.

Thank God, we didn't get hit last night. We got all of the dead out and the rest of the wounded medevaced this morning.

The tanks and Charlie Company swept through the area again. They found six dead gooks, one wounded right in front of where I was.

I had the picture out this morning, the one I took off the gook I killed yesterday. I don't know if it was the man's family or not, but for the first time since I have been in Vietnam these gooks became human beings. I will never forget this. I wanted to keep the picture; I don't know why, but I did. One of the other platoon commanders told me that I had to turn everything in. I don't know why I wanted to keep it, but maybe after the war or sometime I could go find these people and talk to them. It was really strange, because always before when I shot at one of these gooks it was just a gook. You shoot him or he shoots you. Now all of the sudden, here is a guy that I know I killed, and he had what appeared to be a family. It is really sad.

I'm platoon commander now since the lieutenant is out. I hope that I can handle the job. I have really worked hard at trying to lighten up a little bit as a platoon sergeant. So maybe I will be able to deal with this. I don't have too many guys to deal with anyway.

We moved out at about 1200. It was hot; it was really hot. Several of the troops were about to pass out. We finally got set in at about 1730, but nobody seems to know what the hell is going on. Tomorrow we may move up to C4 or maybe to Dong Ha or Quang Tri.

I know that a full platoon is 46 guys and with the guns, corpsman, and everyone else we probably have about 60 guys. I think today when we counted we had 28 guys left in this platoon. That is not very many. I hope that they will get some replacements out here to us.

Earlier tonight I set the LPs in, and one of them went to sleep. We have to set them in single; we can't set them in teams now because we don't have enough people. But the guy was asleep. I think that it was Heim, but I'm not sure. So we will just have to get his butt in here. I'm not going out after him; I just can't do it tonight. I'll send his squad leader. Hopefully, we won't have any trouble from that area.

May 11

I was up at 0600 just standing by. We had some real close air strikes over our next objective. It is a lot closer than I really thought it was. Charlie and Bravo are going to take it. They moved out about 1300. The engineers blew some bunkers, and we moved on up over to the next objective, no contact.

We got on tanks for security and rode them up to C3 Combat Base. We had some hot chow. Then we moved to C2 on trucks. The major in charge of the base is really a neat guy. He sold us some beer. Maybe he is making some money off it; I don't know. But he sold us some beer and we got some decent bunkers for the night, so I don't feel too bad. I guess that we are going to be here a couple of days. They have hot chow twice a day and showers, so it is not really too bad a place to be.

The weather has been hot, so if we stay here for a couple of days, we ought to be OK.

I found out the last thing skipper said just before he was killed. He yelled, "Come here, Pixley, you coward." When he was moving up toward the fight, people tried to tell him to get down, but he must have thought that he was John Wayne. Corbett said that he tried to stop him but he said, "I am a Marine and I am moving up like one." Well, I don't know how many Marines move up like that, but he was taken out like a dead one, so I don't think that it proved anything. I don't know; maybe he was going off the deep end too. But it is crazy. You know, I don't mind fighting, and I'll do what I have to do. But I'm not going to stand up and walk in through the shit like I have a target on my chest. So I feel sorry for him, but he is the one who made the choice and got himself killed. He was always pretty gung ho. Anytime I had anything to do with him he was OK to deal with. Seemed to be a good Marine officer; too bad he had to get himself killed.

May 12

I was up at 0730. I went to chow. It is really nice to get hot chow again for a change.

Lieutenant Casey said that he thinks that we will be here for a couple of days, so we will just kind of hang out and see what happens.

I just hung around today and played cards most of the day. We got some more beer; we still had to pay for it, but at least we are getting some. It is not cold, but it is better than nothing. I also got the word that 1/9 is moving off the line. So maybe they will move us out there. I don't know. But for today we just hung out, drank some beer, played some cards, and took it easy. You never know what tomorrow will bring.

May 13

I was up at 0830. I had some chow and tried to call 1/26 rear and get the company office, but I couldn't get through. I guess the short radio antenna wasn't enough. I put up a whip and got the Six. They were heading toward C3. Maybe they will move us down there; I hope so. A guy here tried to send us on the lines, and I really didn't like that very much. You know, sending our platoon out there is not what I had in mind. I talked to Lieutenant Casey about getting us back with the company. He wasn't too excited about it, but I talked him into calling us back down with them. We got back with the company around 1800.

They have a nice little base here at C2, so we had some steak and beer. The word is now that they are going to chopper us up almost into the DMZ. Then we are going to clear an area along the western edge of Vietnam. So I don't know exactly what is going to happen, but they said that it is supposed to take four days.

We are set in right near this ville, and it was really funny. This is the first time I have been around the gooks when we weren't shooting each other. They are out there selling beer and cakes and just about anything that you want. I suppose you could get a woman if you wanted one, but I am not interested in that right now. So they just walk around like they own the place (I guess they do). Some of the guys bought some stuff, but they warned us to stay away from the bottles of whiskey. Someone said that they put ground-up glass in it, which is really not very good for you.

Huskey, Deschaine, and Markum made it back. Huskey and Deschaine are fine. Markum still has a slight cut across the front of his stomach. It is wrapped up; it doesn't look too bad, but I hope it doesn't get infected. He could very easily get jungle rot in it. So I just told him to keep an eye on it, and we will see. It's nice to have Huskey and Deschaine back. Deschaine can be a pain in the ass sometimes, but he's a damn good Marine and I trust him to watch out for me like I'd watch for him.

These gooks are getting on my nerves, always wanting you to buy their shit. I wonder if I could get away with shooting the next one that comes up to me?

May 14

I was up at 0600 getting ready to chopper out. My platoon will be the last platoon to be choppered out, so we are going to be in the rear of the columns today.

The gooks were back out there selling their shit, and they were selling all kinds of junk. You know, I look at those gooks, old men, women, and children. I just wonder how many of them, if given the chance, would shoot me right in the back.

I got on the chopper at 0940. We flew for about five minutes and landed at 0945. I got the platoon together without any trouble which surprised me. The guys were really listening to me and trying to do what I was asking. We moved out about 600 meters and stopped for four hours. We just sat there, and I hate that when we are out in the middle of the field. Evans [Martin, 2245206] and Adkins, [William, 2309299] were medevaced for heat. It is really hot; the sun was just beating down on us like crazy. Maybe we are not in really good shape.

Nobody seems to know where we are for sure. The maps that they gave us don't seem to cover the area.

Charlie Company took some mortars. I don't know if anybody was wounded or not; I couldn't tell from where we were. I did see some choppers come, though, so maybe they medevaced somebody out. We finally moved out in two columns. We were moving to the south. At about 1600 it started to rain, and man, it really came down. It was just pouring. The gooks didn't help much, either. They fired six rockets in on us. No one from my platoon got hurt though, thank God.

The brush we are moving through is about waist high. Maybe in some places it is up to our shoulders, but we just keep moving through it and heading to the south. We finally got set in at about 1900. It was still raining. This was not a great area to set in. There was just some brush. We dug some holes the best that we could.

We got a new CO today, Captain Daniel (Full name and service number not available), Deschaine's old CO from 1/27 Alpha; he seems to be an OK kind of guy. But I am sure that he is going to try to play Johnny Hard Ass until he gets his feet wet. I hope that he can stay with us for a while, though.

Sitting in here tonight, it doesn't look like it is going to be a real strong position to be in, so I hope that the gooks don't blast us tonight and I can get some sleep.

May 15

I was up at 0400. I had a platoon commander's meeting. They told us that we were going to move out at 0530. It never happened. We sat around until 1030.

You know, it is really an honor to be the platoon commander, but here I am, an E-5 sergeant. I'm not sure that I really like this job. The captain put my platoon on point to move up this hill and take a mortar position. He left it up to me to decide how I wanted to assault the position. He told me where it was; we looked on the map and saw it. So I told the guys to move part way up the hill in columns, and then we kind of spread out. It was sort of like the way we would rabbit hunt with a group of guys back in West Virginia. When we got to the top of the hill and reached the objective, you could see where the gooks had a mortar tube sitting. A few empty cases and a few things were lying around, but there wasn't any mortar position there. I called back down and told the captain. He just told us to bring whatever we found back in. So my first operation as a platoon commander, when I had the platoon by myself, really didn't turn out too bad; at least I didn't get anyone killed.

It really has gotten hot today. The second platoon had two medevacs because of the heat. I didn't see anybody getting wounded.

We finally got the word to move out again at 1230. We met up with Charlie and Bravo Companies. Charlie killed one gook. They found about 100 bunkers. We crossed over the bunkers, and we went down in very carefully, watching for booby traps. I went down into one bunker just to see how good it was; it wasn't worth a shit. I did find a really nice sniper's rifle in a wooden box, still packed in cosmoline. I am going to keep it. I have to take it to the armory when we get back, and I will pick it up before I leave heading back to the world. It looked like it was about a battalion-sized area. We don't know how long the gooks had been there, but there wasn't any sign that they had been there in the last couple of days.

We then moved on down across the little stream and up the hill and set in for the night. It wasn't too bad a place; there was pretty thick jungle around us. We cleared as much as we could by firing M-79s and rifles at the trees. There wasn't room for us on the lines when we got there, so we started to set in behind Bravo Company. Bravo decided to tighten up their lines and let us squeeze in. We got three fighting holes out on the lines, and everybody else was set in the back. I don't really like this idea too much, but just having three fighting holes out there is not bad. Everybody else was safe in the back, so we will set in there. It was about midnight before we got everything squared away.

Just a few minutes ago six gooks just walked into Charlie Company's lines. The Marines on watch killed two of them, and it looks like they think they wounded at least one. They will look for blood trails in the morning. They fired some flares, but the other four got away. But it was really funny.

They said they didn't think that the gooks knew we were there; they just walked right up to the holes. They were just strolling along like they were on a Sunday walk and walked right into our lines. Thank God the guys were awake. I am going to try to get some sleep now. It's 0200, so I don't know how much sleep I am going to get tonight, but I'll give it a try. I think that this job is getting to me. You know, it is a worry when you are responsible for this many men. The decisions that you make could get them killed. I will be glad when Lieutenant Asmus gets back. This job is OK, but it is getting me down.

May 16

I was up at 0600 getting ready to move back to the area where we got on the choppers. That is one thing about this stupid war I don't understand. We go out and clear a section; it looks like it is going to be secure, then they move us back to where we started from.

As we were moving down this hill, Bravo got hit by a rocket or recoilless rifle. I don't know what hit them, but you could hear it go off. They had one killed and four wounded. They were really worried about bringing in a chopper to medevac the wounded, but they got them out OK.

We moved up past H&S Company and took the point. We moved in to the area just before dark. We are sitting in the same area that we were in before. We don't have real good bunkers but at least a place that we can fight from. We had some hot chow and a couple of beers. It wasn't too bad. I had a couple snorts from a bottle that I bought from the gooks and have been hiding. It didn't look like it had any glass in it.

We are going in to Quang Tri by CH-53s tomorrow, they say. We will stay there a couple of days, and then we will get back in the bush.

May 17

We did some serious traveling today. I was up at 0600 and had some chow. I kind of policed up the area. We just kept our eyes on the bush but didn't have any problems. At 1030 they loaded us on CH-53s and flew us into Quang Tri. We got into Quang Tri and set in just beside the air strip where they let us off. We sat there until 1400. When the last of the troops got in, we went over to 1/26 rear and got some utilities and boots. Several of the guys' boots were shot, and we needed some utilities. They got torn up from being in the bush so much. Climbed on some C-130s at 1530 and headed for Da Nang. We landed, got on trucks, and went out behind Hill 327, a place called the Rock Quarry. It is not too bad a place; it's a pretty secure area. Of course, Da Nang still reminds me of the first day that I was here. It looks like landing in Pittsburgh.

I called Darrel Pennington, and he came out for chow and a little BS. We sat around talking; it was nice to see him again. He has got this nice cushy job here in the rear, but I guess when you get to be gunnery sergeant you can do that kind of stuff.

I didn't have any real scoop to pass on to the troops or anything that I heard here today. It looks like we will be here for a few days. Then we will be back out in the bush again. Until then, I'm going to drink all the beer I can get my hands on and have a good time.

May 18

It was a typical day in the rear. We just sat around and didn't do much. I checked on everybody's gear to make sure that they had plenty of ammunition. I talked to each one of the right guides and made sure that they knew where to get the stuff they needed.

The skipper left. We couldn't get any scoop; I don't know where he went.

After chow I felt pretty good. I had nice hot chow; we have a nice little mess hall here. It's just like being back home.

All of the staff NCOs and COs got liberty; we could go wherever we wanted and do whatever we wished to do as long as we are back by 0800 tomorrow morning. Henson, Hicks [Richard S., 2131715], and I went down to the Thunderbird Club; it was really a pretty neat bar.

We met some officer's paige; I don't remember what his name was. He took us down to his hooch, and we spent the night there. We had to wrestle with some guys to get a place to sleep, but it wasn't too bad. It was really an outstanding hooch. They had a tape recorder set up and a really outstanding turntable. They fixed us up with some chow and gave us a rack. It was really an outstanding place. But you know, it was really strange, here were these guys who are here in Da Nang at this nice cushy rear base, and they were really taken by us. I didn't realize it at first, but all they wanted to do was hear stories about what it was like in the bush. We are cleaned up; we had showers and everything, but they knew we had been in the bush. The guys that have been in the bush know what is going on. They also have that stare; I can't explain it, but we all have it. Of course, we all kind of stretched the truth a few times and told them some tales. It was a good night. I had a lot of fun. I bet I sleep like a baby tonight.

May 19

I got up at 0630, had to be back to the platoon area by 0800. We made it with no problem. The guys down at the place that we stayed at last night were all right. But it is still strange that all they wanted to do was hear about what was going on in the bush.

We got back here with no problem by 0800 and just sat around most of the day. Alpha pulled out for someplace. I don't know where they are going, and nobody seemed to know. The skipper wasn't around, so I don't know what happened.

The 3rd Platoon was sent over to an artillery battery. They said that they needed more security over there. They were gone about two hours, but they came back. We are supposed to go out to some LZ tomorrow. I don't know where that is going to be, but it looks like we are heading back for the bush.

I went down and watched a flick down on Main Side tonight. It wasn't too bad; it was a John Wayne movie made probably back in the 40s someplace. But it was a pretty good movie. I enjoyed it. I am going to sleep good tonight. This will be my last night in the rack, I'll bet.

May 20

I was up at 0400. I ran into Dunbar (full name and service number not available) and met some E-5 named Davis (full name and service number not available) at chow. They are a couple of pretty good guys. We sat around and shot the bull a little bit.

We went down to a recon LZ at 0930 to be on Bald Eagle. They gave us some kool-aid while we were sitting on the LZ. The way this operation works, we are going to sit down here by the CH-46s all day. If recon or somebody spots twenty or so gooks, they will load us on the choppers and we are going to fly out there and shoot up the world and take care of things. We will secure the area, do whatever we have to do, and then fly back. It doesn't look like too bad a deal.

At about 1100 it was getting hot, so they took us up to the club, where we just laid around all day drinking Cokes. It was pretty nice. We got the Cokes for free; they were cold, even. So it wasn't too bad. They said that we are back there again tomorrow. So this is what we have to do for the next few days. It won't be bad for a few days, but I think that if this continues for any long period of time, the troops and myself are going to get pretty bored.

I was back in our area at 1600. I watched the movie in our area tonight. The guy running the projector was funnier to watch than the movie. He had a hell of a time getting it going. He didn't seem to know how to run it. I had a real slow day. Good night to sleep.

May 21

I was up at 0400. I made it to chow and headed for the LZ. We just sat around there until 1100, when we got the word that it was time to move out. Recon had spotted some gooks. They flew us out about 15 minutes. The choppers fired their M-60s to help secure some kind of an LZ. We landed and let 3rd Platoon out. 3rd Platoon took out after a couple VC but couldn't catch them. We moved on up toward 3rd Platoon's position. They crossed our front and moved in to check out a ville on our left. They didn't find anything. I called the choppers to pick us up. As the choppers were coming back in, they took some small-arms fire from their right rear. We returned fire, and we fired a few mortars at them. It wasn't long afterwards that two Hueys came in and really worked out on that area. I don't know if the gooks were still there, probably not, but at least we fired some ammunition at them.

3rd Platoon had one man wounded but not too seriously; he got shot in the hip. My platoon was the last one out after the skipper left, and gunny stayed with me. We just messed around while we were waiting for the choppers to come back and get us. We took some potshots at a few birds. We tried to hit a chicken down in the ville, but none of us were good enough shots to hit it. They flew us out to a place called An Hou and then into Da Nang. We got back to the area at about 1800, had some mail, and went to a flick. I got a letter from Mom, and she said everything seems to be OK at home. So I'm really glad to hear that.

It rained while I was at the flick, and my poncho liner that I had left out got soaked. That pissed me off, but I'll live with it.

May 22

I was up at 0630. I went to chow and then headed for the LZ. We are on standby for the Army with Bravo Company today.

This was the third day of standing at attention for colors; really makes me feel good. You know, it has been a long time since I've heard a band play or listened to the music or seen the flag raised. You really don't appreciate that flag until you fight for it. It was really neat. I spend almost every minute that the song is being played and the flag is going up thinking about being back at Khe Sanh. When we would wake up in the morning, the first thing that we would do was look to see if the flag was still flying. If it was flying we knew we still had control of the base. It really makes you feel good, really proud.

I got to take half of the platoon down to the Eleventh Mortar for a few beers and a flick. It wasn't too bad; the troops were happy about it. I didn't stay with them; Henson and I left them and went over to the Thunderbird Club.

I fell in love with this lady named Hoa; what a chick. She can't sing worth a shit, but after she did a song, she came over and sat at our table. She doesn't speak real good English, but who cares. Boy, what I could do to her if I just had half a chance. She is really a fine-looking chick. I think I am in love again.

May 23

I was up at 0500 and went down to the LZ. I just sat around all day. They brought the troops hot chow down again, which was kind of nice. We came back to the area at 1400.

Gago, R. (full name and service number not available) is coming to our platoon. I went through ITR with him. He seemed like a pretty decent guy. It will work out pretty good, I think. He is an E-5, but senior to me. He is going to be platoon sergeant, and Staff Sergeant Tolentino, [Claren, 1268075] is going to be platoon commander for right now. I will be back to right guide. It's OK with me. I am just ready to sit back and let somebody else run the show for a while. I'm tired; it has really gotten to me, being a platoon commander.

We went with the platoon over to Thunderbird Club, but the electricity went off, so we couldn't stay. We went back over to Eleven Mortars and had a few beers. I didn't stay with them. I went up to see Pennington, and he was heading for a strip show over at the hospital, so I went with him and saw a great strip show.

I came back to our area at 2315. I am going to get some sleep, and I think that it will be a good night's sleep.

May 24

It started out just the same as any other day. I was up at 0500 and down at the LZ. I just sat there in the shade of the choppers all day. They brought some hot chow down, and we were back in the area at 1330. Gago is doing a good job. He is trying to get to know the guys and working with them pretty well. He has taken a lot of weight off my shoulders. It is really nice to have somebody else that can help make some decisions around here.

At about 1700 we got the word to go to the club. We no more than got the word when they changed it right quick and told us to get saddled up. We are going out to a downed chopper. I got the guys ready to go and headed for the LZ. Then the skipper said nope, it's off.

So the club run was back on. But by the time we got everything squared away, it was 1930. We got to the club, and almost everybody was drunk anyway. But that was alright; we got to visit and drink a few beers. I enjoyed it, even though I'm still the platoon commander. I won't be for long. I felt more like one of the guys again. We came back here at 2330. We'll just go to sleep and see what happens tomorrow.

May 25

The same old shit, just a different day. I was up at 0500 and down at the LZ by 0600. I knew this would be a drag before very long. The first few days were kind of nice, getting to go to the club and seeing some round eyes, that kind of thing was nice. But now it is getting to be a real drag. They sent us back to the area at 1400.

They had a club run, but I didn't go. I stayed back and was going to watch a flick. They couldn't find the projector. It is typical of the way things are run around here. It was 2200 before they found the projector, so I only got to watch about half a flick before they called platoon commanders up.

We are going out on a four-day operation tomorrow, out toward An Hoe.

Staff Sergeant Tolentino will be back in the morning, so I'll go back to right guide. It will be nice to have someone else making decisions for the platoon. He was at the club tonight, but he was pretty drunk, so I really didn't talk to him. I don't know, he seemed a little bit cocky to me. A few days in the bush will take that out of him.

This will be my last night as a platoon commander. I hope nothing happens that I have to take the troops out.

May 26

I was up at 0530 and missed breakfast. We loaded on trucks and headed out south of Da Nang. We got out there, unloaded, and sat there. It took us about an hour to get set up, and we sat there for about four hours. We then crossed a river on a ferry and set in for the night.

It really poured down the rain. I was lucky that Green brought a poncho so I was able to get under that with him a little bit, so it wasn't too bad. I lost mine before we came to Da Nang. We stayed pretty dry.

Tolentino couldn't read a map with thrust points on it, so I had to show him how to do it. I guess he had never learned how to do it when he was wherever he was before here. So I showed him how to do it; he caught on pretty quickly. I think that he will do pretty good. He said that he won a silver star for killing eleven gooks, but you know how that story goes. He doesn't know me, so I could tell him I received one for killing twelve.

Gago couldn't sleep. The bugs were driving him crazy. He hasn't been in the bush for very long. Of course, the rest of us are all used to it. We do have a little bit of lotion that we can put on to keep the bugs away. It doesn't work very well. He just can't stand it; the bugs were really getting to him, so he will just have to sleep the best that he can tonight.

May 27

I was up at 0430. We moved out at 0530. We moved about 2500 meters. We came into this ville; we were moving pretty slow. We found some fighting holes, so I burned down a haystack. We found some other junk. It looked like gook stuff, so we burned down about half of the ville. I was hoping that we could find some NVA gear. I would kill a couple of the women. I knew I would kill anybody that moved in front of me, and I mean anybody. If it got in front of me, it was dead.

I came up to this bunker. I saw someone jump down into it as we were coming through the ville. I pulled the pin and threw a grenade down in the hole, and it went off. I heard some yelling and screaming. So I just threw another one in. There may have been women and children down there, but I didn't care. I am tired of seeing people killed—my friends killed. These damn gooks, all I can think about is killing them. I am tired of this place. We kept sweeping on through the ville and I kept hoping we would see some gooks to kill.

Deschaine's squad found some ammo. So we went back and burned the whole damn ville down. We killed their pigs and chickens, and anything that moved, we shot. If any gooks had come out of their holes, I would have loved to have killed them too. 3rd Platoon took some sniper fire, so they pulled back. We called in arty and air. They leveled the whole damn ville. I didn't care who was in it or what was in it. They all deserved to die.

I got a couple shots off at one guy, but I don't know if I hit him or not. I was aiming at him. That's one thing about a round from an M-16; you never know where it is going for sure.

We moved up on this hill off behind the ville and set in for the night. A chopper tried to come in and resupply us, but there was too much sniper fire, so he pulled away. We didn't get any chow tonight.

It was really a strange day. I'll tell you, I felt really hateful all day. I have never experienced anything like this. I don't know if it was sitting on the LZ so many days, or what it was, maybe being in the bush too long. But I would have killed anything. I didn't care what it was; I would have shot it today. You know, I am tired of seeing my friends get killed and wounded and stupid things happen. I am just tired of this war altogether. If anybody messes with me tonight, they are dead.

May 28

I was up at 0400 for radio watch. Deschaine took a dive on radio watch. I don't know what time it was, but they got me up to take care of it.

At about 2300 it started to rain, and I got soaked. I just can't stand this place.

The LP went to sleep, so I threw some rocks at him, trying to get him to wake up, and he finally did.

I was really hoping that they would resupply us this morning, but they didn't get it done. I haven't eaten but one meal in three days, and I am out of smokes. Nothing pisses me off worse than to be out of smokes. But they didn't get us resupplied in the morning. They told us to get ready to move out, and they would resupply us later on during the day.

We moved out about 300 meters and stopped. We were moving along this rice paddy. I was walking up on the dikes. Corbett told me I was going to get hit; we could see rounds hitting in the water and hear the AKs going off. I told him I didn't give a shit. If I got hit and didn't die I'd be in a nice dry hospital bed tonight. If I got hit and died I'd probably be in hell tonight and wouldn't care. If I didn't get hit I would be sleeping in dry clothes tonight.

When we stopped, we watched a couple of A-4s drop napalm on this little hill about 800 meters in front of us. We just sat there for about two hours watching it happen. Then they decided to move up.

My platoon was in the middle. The 2nd Platoon was on our left and 3rd Platoon was on our right. We moved in to the base of this hill. The brush was pretty thick, but it wasn't really bad. We got the word to move out to assault the hill and take it, so we jumped up and started across. We killed a couple of gooks as we went across. I got one of the bastards. We were on line, the whole platoon. We moved up the hill and down the other side. There were some graves in the rice paddy lying right out in front of us, and a couple of the gooks were hiding behind them. So we took some potshots at them with the M-79s. Deschaine was pointing the thing almost straight up in the air. Corbett was doing the same. They were dropping the M-79 rounds right behind graves. I couldn't tell if we hit any gooks, but I'll bet we pissed off the gooks in the graves. Then we got the word to pull back.

2nd Platoon and 3rd Platoon hadn't pulled out, so we were basically surrounded. I checked, and nobody was hurt. I called in and told them that we had reached our objective, and they said, "OK. You have to pull back." We went back up the hill and back down the other side. Back where we started from.

When we were coming back down the hill we could see the gooks had already closed up their trench line where we had come through. It was just like shooting ducks in a barrel. We were shooting them right in the back. They were facing away from us and didn't know we were coming down on them. We secured that area, and I called over to 2nd Platoon and told their platoon sergeant to stop firing straight ahead and I would clear the trench line in front of him. I got one of the guys behind me to protect my back, and I started through the trench line. I had gone maybe 10 feet when a gook stood up and I killed him. They were all looking out to their front and I was coming at them from the side. He went down in the hole, so I jumped in on top of him. I was going to cut his ear off. As I was dropping into the hole, out of the corner of my eye I saw another gook stand up, so I switched magazines in my rifle and stood up to fire at him. I was firing directly down the trench line, when out of the corner of my eye, I saw a rifle aimed at me. I whirled as fast as I could; the bullet went through my hand, through my rifle stock, and hit me in the shoulder. I was down! In that instant I looked up in front of me at a vision of millions and millions of people. They were standing in a big crowd; the ones closest to me were dressed in normal clothes. They were all staring up toward this white cloud-like area. I guessed it was God. I knew then I was going to die. I thought of my mother and how my death would affect her. I told myself I wasn't going to die in this fucking hole. I picked up my rifle just as I saw a gook crawling down the trench toward me. My right hand was no good; three of my fingers were just hanging on by skin. I cradled my M-16 in my left arm and put it on full automatic. I held it with my left hand and laid it on the bottom of the trench floor. When the gook got close to me, I pulled the trigger. The rounds were going through him and hitting the gook behind him. I knew then I was going to make it.

The round that hit me glanced off my flak jacket. My shoulder hurt worse than anything else at first. It felt like I had been kicked by a mule. I knew that half of my hand was cut off, so I pulled what was left of it up against me to try and stop the bleeding and started yelling for somebody to come and help me.

I realized I was in this hole, lying on top of a dead gook, and couldn't get down lower in the hole. At about that time, Corbett moved up with his M-79 and fired into the machine gun bunker that had me pinned down. He secured it well enough that he could get me out. One of the guys jumped down in the hole, picked me up, and moved me back away from the trench line. He moved me over close to the LZ. A Corpsman came up and wrapped my hand and gave me a shot. I'm not sure what was in that shot, but in about five minutes I was ready to go back into the fight. While I was waiting for my chopper some of the guys came by to get my ammunition and things I wouldn't need for a while. I gave away my K-bar and rifle. I knew I was out of here.

I sat there in the LZ for what seemed like a long time. I wasn't one of the most critically wounded guys. There were some guys a whole lot worse than me. They made me wait for a third chopper. By the time the chopper got there I was really starting to worry. The bleeding hadn't stopped and my blood was running out of the bandage. They finally loaded me on a chopper, and just as we took off we were hit. I saw the bullet holes appear in the side of the chopper. I thought, "Wouldn't this be the shits, get wounded and then shot down." Nothing was hit that would bring us down—we kept flying, flying me out of this damn war.

It was really strange. When we got into Da Nang, we got off the chopper. Some of the guys were being carried; a Corpsman came over and kind of put his one arm under me and tried to help me get in. I felt really weak. We walked into this big Quonset hut. There was nothing in it except poles against the wall. As we came in, the Corpsman pulled these cot standards out and set the cots up on them, and I laid down on top of the thing. They set them up just as each wounded man came to that spot. The first Corpsman came in and started right at my boots. He cut every bit of my shoes, pants, shirt, everything right off me. He just laid them open. He didn't take them out from under me; he just laid them open. He took everything out of my pockets. I had two empty magazines and my diary. He asked me if I wanted to keep the diary; I said yes, and he put it in a plastic bag and hooked it to my cot. He then moved on to the next guy. The next corpsman came, and he had a clipboard. He took my name, rank, and all that kind of stuff and wrote down something about where I was hit. He hung the clipboard on the cot and moved on to the next guy. The next Corpsman came up and unbandaged my hand and looked at it. It was really funny. There was a big dead fly lying right on top of it. There was a doctor who came over and looked at my hand and said, "Take him to X-ray." So they took me in X-ray—me, my cot, my clipboard, and my diary. In the meantime, they had given me a couple more shots. The Corpsman in the field had given me a shot to kill the pain. The Corpsman gave me another shot when I got in there. So I was about half asleep. After the X-ray, the doctor told me that he was going to cut everything off except my little finger and my ring finger. Everything else would be cut off. You know, it was strange, but I didn't care. I was alive. And my sexual parts were the one thing that I worried most about getting blown off, and they were still intact. I figured, hey, I can get by with only one hand.

They took me into an operating room, and the doctor gave me a local anesthetic. He raised my arm and stuck me with what looked like a wee little tiny needle and a great big syringe. He started twisting the thing around in my arm pit after he just jammed it in there. He said that when I felt the tingle in my fingers to tell him, so I told him that I felt it. He gave me the shot and laid my hand down on the table. There was a board sticking out from under the piece of rubber I was lying on, and that is what they laid my hand on. It wasn't a real fancy place. I thought I would get to watch as the doctor cut on me, but they put this cardboard box over my head. It had cutouts for my shoulders, and it said Kelloggs right across the front of the box. They pulled the sheet over the top of my head.

I was about half asleep, but I could feel them pulling and tugging and so forth on my hand. I mean, there was no pain or anything, but I could just feel the grinding and the pulling as they pulled parts of my hand off, my fingers, I guessed. So I was lying there just about half asleep. All of the sudden, I could feel the pain coming up my arm. I sat up, and about that time, they put something over my face and put me to sleep.

When I woke up, I had a cast on my hand, or part of a cast with tubes coming out of it. I looked, and I could see three fingertips sticking out of the end of the cast. The doctor came in and told me that he had taken off my middle finger and had sewn my first finger and thumb back on. He had used some clips to pull the rest of my hand back together. They didn't know how it would work but he wanted to save as much of my hand as he could. They had a tube coming out the side draining it. I would be going back to the States, and they would see what they could do for me back there. Maybe it would stay or maybe they would have to take the rest of it off. But at least at this point I had three fingers and a thumb.

This Corpsman came in then and told me that I had to make a choice about where I wanted to go. From the choices that he gave me, because I thought the naval hospital in Bethesda, Maryland, was probably the closest one to home, that was the one that I chose.

Then Lieutenant Asmus and Heath came in to see me. And we talked a little bit. It was really nice to see Lieutenant Asmus. He was up and walking around. He was going back to the company as XO. He had orders for me to report to a map-reading outfit. As a sergeant I was allowed to turn down the orders once, and I had. I would have raised enough hell to stay with my platoon this time but I was wounded and didn't have to. I wasn't sure why Heath wasn't back with his platoon. I knew he had been in Bangkok on R&R, so I had a pretty good idea why he was hanging around the rear. I told them that I was going back to the world and I would really miss them both. I hope that everything went alright with them.

It was about 1600 when I got shot, and they took me over to the air terminal and put me on a plane at about 2400. I am on my way back to the world. I am alive. I am shot, but I am not hurt too badly. Thank God I made it, and I am going home.

May 29

At 0100 they loaded us on a C-141 and headed for the States. They have racks on this thing that are four tiers high. They look like they are about five deep. So there are a good many wounded people on here. Then they have some seats in the front for people who are ambulatory and for people, I guess, who are just on for the ride. I was on the top bunk, and the air conditioner was blowing right on me. I don't know if it is supposed to be heat or air conditioning, but it is cold.

We landed in Japan, put some guys off, and picked some other guys up. I was looking out the back, and it was raining. We took off again, and the next thing I knew, we landed in Alaska. They didn't open the back doors this time, so I didn't get to see out, but they did unload some guys there.

During the flight a nurse came by every once in a while and asked me how I was doing. I was really hurting, so she would give something for pain. She said I could get hooked on the painkillers, but I didn't give a shit, my hand really hurt. A couple times I asked her for them, she wouldn't give them to me. If I could have gotten down off that rack, I would have kicked her ass. When I did get one it put me to sleep.

I was really feeling sorry for myself. You know, Mr. Stud of the world who loves the girls and wants to be loved by them, and here I am, wounded. I thought, "Man, I am going to be crippled. Even though it is the hand that, when I am dancing with a girl, will be behind her back, I am still crippled." I was really feeling sorry for myself. There were a lot of guys moaning and crying and stuff on the plane. But a guy was lying across from me clear against the other bulkhead of the plane. He rolled over, and his hand was cut off right above his wrist. I thought, "Bullshit, Oyster, you will never feel sorry for yourself again, ever." I mean, at least if I only have two fingers, which would be the least that they said that I would have, I am better off than this guy. I will never feel sorry for myself again. I chose to be here. I volunteered to go to Vietnam, and I served my country. And if I am crippled, I will live with it.

I went back to sleep.

May 29 AGAIN

Coming back from Vietnam, I got two May 29s.

We landed at Andrews Air Force Base at about 2000. I couldn't believe it when the Corpsmen got on the plane to take me off. They wore such starch white uniforms. I couldn't believe it. It was just unbelievable. They were so clean and nice and everything. I hadn't seen anything that clean in a long time.

Some boot lieutenant climbed into the ambulance as the Corpsmen were loading me up. He wanted to know if there was anything that he could do to help me. He gave me a smoke, and he said what a great job we are doing in Vietnam. I told him thanks, but I wanted to kick his ass. You know, I thought, "Here you are, you boot lieutenant; you don't know shit from shinola about what's going on over there. Here you are, being such a hot dog." I guess he was trying to be nice, or maybe just doing his job.

We were driving on the beltway around D.C. The Corpsman held my head up so that I could see out. I couldn't believe all the lights. The red and white lights from the cars, I just never thought much about them before. There were all the lights from cars and the lights in windows, and lights from everywhere. It was really beautiful, and I started to cry. I couldn't stop crying. I am so lucky, so lucky to be alive. There are so many guys who are dead. And I just cried; it was really beautiful.

We got to the hospital, and it was really something. This girl came up to me, I guess she was a nurse or Corpsman or something. She said that I could call anyplace in the United States or anyplace that I wanted to call. They gave me a free three-minute phone call. I got three free minutes. I wanted to call Mom and Dad. I gave the girl the number and she dialed it for me. When Mom answered the phone, I said, "Hi, Mom, I'm back in the world." I didn't know what happened to her; I don't know if she passed out or just dropped the phone. Dad grabbed the phone, and I said, "Hey, man, I am back in the world." Of course, Mom wanted to know the whole story and what had happened to me. I just kept emphasizing the fact that I wasn't hurt bad and it was nothing real major, that I lost a finger and part of my hand, but there wasn't really anything wrong with me that bad. We talked for the three minutes, and Mom said they would be down to see me tomorrow.

The girl came back after I had hung up the phone and took the phone back for me. I thought, "Man, she is the most beautiful girl that I have ever seen in my life." I don't know what she really looked like, but you know when I first saw her, she was really beautiful.

After the phone call, they took me upstairs. They are going to put me in a ward, and they said that they had to clean me up first. Well I had no idea what I looked like. They got me off the gurney and stood me up in front of a mirror. Of course, I was stark naked. The only part of me that was clean that you could see was from the cast up to my elbow. Everything else was covered with blood and mud. I had mud and blood ratted in my hair, and I had about a five- or six-day growth of beard. I really was one scum bucket. They put me down in this bathtub, and the Corpsman washed and cleaned me up. Boy, it sure felt good to have that warm water on me. They said that I could have anything that I wanted to eat, so I said, "Man, I want a steak and some ice cream." They got me cleaned up and took me up and put me in my bunk in the hospital ward. They brought me up the chow, but I couldn't eat it. I had like one bite of the steak and a little bit of ice cream.

It's now time to go to sleep. I just can't handle it anymore. I'm tired. All that I can say is "Thank God, I'm alive." I see a lot of guys here in the ward, and you can't really see who they are. It's kind of dark in here. But I know that there are a bunch of other wounded soldiers and Marines in here. And we are all lucky, really really lucky, to be alive.

The war is over for me. I know I'll never forget it and the men I came to know more than just as military acquaintances. I loved those guys and they loved me. What we did together, we can only share with each other. I am so lucky to have known men like Corbett, Lt. Asmus, Deschaine, Shortround, and all the other guys I was with. May God be with them.

EPILOGUE

I remained in Bethesda Naval Hospital for eight months. I was retired from the Marine Corps with a 60% disability in 1971. I went to Fairmont State College, Fairmont, West Virginia, and received my undergraduate degree in education. I married Betty Jean Nightingale and have four children, Michael, Brian, Gregory, and Erin. I received my masters degree from West Virginia University, Morgantown, West Virginia, in 1980. I have been a teacher since 1972, currently working with students with disabilities.

I served seven months in Vietnam. I returned to my hometown of Chester, West Virginia, to a hero's welcome. I have no real problems from serving in Vietnam. I volunteered to go and have only the highest regard for my country. Although I don't agree with the way my government handled the war, I would go again if the need arose.

GLOSSARY

175 mm U.S.-built self-propelled gun

A-1E Sky Warrior Small prop-driven airplane used for close-in support

A-4 Skyhawk A single-seat lightweight jet attack bomber.

AK-47 Soviet-manufactured 7.62 mm assault rifle, standard issue for NVA

Alpha The letter A in the Marine Corps phonetic alphabet used to spell out words in radio conversations. A Company could also be known as Alpha Company.

Amtrack Personnel carrier

AO Area of Operations

APC Armored personnel carrier

Arty Slang for artillery

ARVN Army, of the republic of Vietnam

B-52 Stratofortress Eight-engine, swept-wing heavy jet bomber

Bald Eagle Operation outside the base using helicopters

BAS Battalion aid station

Bravo The letter B in the Marine Corps phonetic alphabet

Bru Mountain tribe living near Khe Sanh

Bush Slang for the jungle

Cattle cars Slang for troop carriers

C-4 Plastic explosive

C-123 Providers Small twin-engine cargo plane

C-130 Air Force Hercules transport aircraft

C-rations Canned meals for use by combat troops in the field
CAC Combined Action Company
Caribou Small twin-engine cargo plane
Cannabera Jet engine-driven light bomber
CH-46 Sea Knight U.S.-built, medium-transport, twin-turbine helicopter
CH-53 Sikorsky heavy cargo helicopter (Sea Stallion)
Charlie The letter C in the Marine Corps phonetic alphabet--also slang for Viet Cong
Chicom Chinese Communist
Chieu Hoi Vietnamese phrase meaning "open arms." A U.S. program encouraging enemy troops to defect and become scouts and interpreters for Allied forces
Chopper Helicopter
Civvies Slang for civilian clothes
Claymore Antipersonnel mine that spews out 700 steel balls in a 60-degree arc---lethal up to 50 meters
Click kilometer (1000 meters)
Cobra The nickname for the AH-1G gunship that replaced the B-model Huey gunship in 1967.
CO Commanding officer
Conx box A large metal storage box
Co Roc Mountain from which the NVA-launched rockets
CP Command post
Delta The letter D in the Marine Corps phonetic alphabet
DMZ The Demilitarized zone, where North and South Vietnam were partitioned at the 17th parallel.
Di-di Slang term for running away in combat
EM club Enlisted man's club
F4-Phantom Jet fighter plane
F-8 Crusader Attack bomber
Finger Area of hill sloping away from the main hill
Field of fire Area in front of a fighting position that you can cover from your position

Flak jacket Armored vest worn by U.S. forces for protection
FO Forward observer
FOB Forward observation base
Frag Fragmentation grenade
Fragging Getting screwed—killing someone of senior rank
Gunny Slang for gunnery sergeant
Hand grenade, M-26 U.S.-manufactured, hand-thrown bomb
H and I Heat and incendiary artillery rounds
Hooch Slang term for a Vietnamese farmer's dwelling. Also, a short-term sleeping spot
Howitzer 105 U.S.-built, towed, general-purpose light artillery piece
Howitzer 155 U.S.-built, towed, medium artillery piece mounted on two wheels
Huey Bell UH-1E attack and transport utility helicopter
Humping Walking from one place to another in the bush
ITR Infantry training regiment
Jack-offs Hand-released flares
KIA Killed in action
Lifers Career Marines
LP Listening post
LZ Landing zone
M-16 U.S.-manufactured 5.56 mm rifle, standard weapon for most infantrymen
M-60 U.S.-manufactured 7.62 mm light general-purpose machine gun that fires 600 rounds per minute
M-79 U.S.-manufactured 40 mm single-shot grenade launcher
MCI Marine Corps Institute
Medevac Medical evacuation, usually performed by helicopter
Mite Small four-wheeled machine used in place of a jeep
Mortar, 60 mm U.S.-built, smooth-bore, muzzle-loaded, single-shot, high–angle-of-fire weapon, easily carried

Mortar, 81 mm U.-. built, smooth-bore, muzzle-loaded, single-shot, high–angle-of-fire weapon

Mo gas Jet fuel

Napalm Jellied incendiary used in air strikes

NCO non-commissioned officer

NPC The money used by the Americans in Vietnam

NVA North Vietnamese Army—generic term for any soldier or group of soldiers from the North

Otters Tracked vehicle used as transport in wet areas

Platoon minus A platoon without one squad

Police call/police up Slang for cleaning up the area

Puff (the Magic Dragon) U.S. Air Force World War II-era twin-engine C-47 Gooneybird aircraft, renamed AC-47 and equipped with three rapid-fire 7.62 mm Gatling guns that could expend 6,000 rounds per minute

Punji pit Hole dug by Viet Cong with sharp sticks sticking upward usually covered with feces and used as a trap

Rack Slang for bed

Recoilless rifle, 106mm U.S.-built, single=shot, recoilless, breech-loaded weapon

Rocket, 122 mm Soviet-built, four-piece, fin-stabilized 9-foot rocket

Roundeye Slang for girls other than Asian

RPG Soviet rocket-propelled grenade launcher that fired an 82 mm warhead, used by the NVA as an antipersonnel weapon

R&R Rest and recuperation

Recon Reconnaissance

Running lights Slang for eyes

Seabag Large bag for carrying personal gear

Seabees U.S. Navy Construction Battalion

Six-by (6-by) Large military truck

Skipper Slang for commanding officer

Sparrow hawk Short operation outside of the base

Stand to First thing in the morning

Starlight scope Device that makes seeing at night possible

TAD Temporary additional duty

Tanglefoot wire Barbed wire strung in different ways to form a barrier

TET Vietnamese lunar new year

The six (Delta six) Term for company commander

Thompson Sub-machine gun

Tipsy Device used to pick up sounds through the earth

Top Slang for 1st sergeant

VC Viet Cong

Water buffalo A work animal for the Vietnamese

WIA Wounded in action

XO Executive officer, second in command

Ville Village

CPSIA information can be obtained at www.ICGtesting.com
Printed in the USA
LVOW040958180312

273585LV00002B/81/P